Matthew Arnold

St. Paul and Protestantism:

With other essays

Matthew Arnold

St. Paul and Protestantism:
With other essays

ISBN/EAN: 9783337810122

Printed in Europe, USA, Canada, Australia, Japan

Cover: Foto ©ninafisch / pixelio.de

More available books at **www.hansebooks.com**

ST. PAUL

AND

PROTESTANTISM

WITH OTHER ESSAYS

BY

MATTHEW ARNOLD

POPULAR EDITION

LONDON
SMITH, ELDER, & CO., 15 WATERLOO PLACE
1892

PREFACE.

TIME MOVES and Opinion moves with it; moves to-day, how fast, how sweepingly! I turn over the pages of *St. Paul and Protestantism*, written some sixteen years ago; what has become of the doctrines of unscriptural Protestantism criticised in it? Sixteen years ago the movement of time and change had indeed reached them, even in this country. But now it has so prevailed over them that the careful exhibition and criticism of them, in the pages which follow, seems almost a waste of labour. Where are now those great and grave doctrines which so possessed the thoughts of religious England formerly? Where is the doctrine of predestination?—gone! Where are the doctrines of original sin, imputed righteousness, and justification by faith? where are they, not as tenets to be formally professed, but as doctrines to fill and form man's mind and soul? They are fast going. Where, too, is the 'Dissidence of Dissent,' with its 'spirit of watchful jealousy?' The Liberals of the nadir still hope to conjure with it; but what open mind does not now perceive its narrowness, poverty, and sterility?

What remains growing and puissant, then, of those factors in our religious condition which are in the following pages mentioned? Undoubtedly growth and power, at this moment, are chiefly with that revulsion to which notice is there directed : the revulsion of man's intellect from the results in which his invincible religious impulse has asserted itself, because of the audacious assumptions and gross inaccuracies with which his account of those results is intermingled.

This remains, this grows and gains strength. There also remains, undoubtedly, the fundamental and indestructible object of Christianity,—the figure and influence of Jesus. But the presentation of this in the arrangement imposed on it by the received Catholic and Protestant theology, filled and informed by mankind's familiar fancies of miracle, blood, bargain and appeasement, to-day endangers it. And therefore that prodigy of religious insight, by which St. Paul in the first age disengaged it from those fancies, has become of quite inestimable importance. Hardly, perhaps, can there be at present attempted a more beneficial service to religion, than the true criticism of this great and misunderstood author.

CONTENTS.

	PAGE
ST. PAUL AND PROTESTANTISM	1
PURITANISM AND THE CHURCH OF ENGLAND . .	81
MODERN DISSENT	123
A COMMENT ON CHRISTMAS	147

ST. PAUL

AND

PROTESTANTISM.

I.

M. RENAN sums up his interesting volume on St. Paul by saying :—' After having been for three hundred years, thanks to Protestantism, the Christian doctor *par excellence*, Paul is now coming to an end of his reign.' All through his book M. Renan is possessed with a sense of this close relationship between St. Paul and Protestantism. Protestantism has made Paul, he says; Pauline doctrine is identified with Protestant doctrine; Paul is a Protestant doctor, and the counterpart of Luther. M. Renan has a strong distaste for Protestantism, and this distaste extends itself to the Protestant Paul. The reign of this Protestant is now coming to an end, and such a consummation evidently has M. Renan's approval.

St. Paul is now coming to an end of his reign. Precisely the contrary, I venture to think, is the judgment to which a true criticism of men and of things, in our own country at any rate, leads us. The Protestantism which has so used and abused St. Paul is coming to an end; its organisations, strong and active as they look, are touched with the finger of death; its fundamental ideas, sounding forth still every week from thousands of pulpits, have in them no significance and no power for the progressive thought of humanity. But the reign of the real St. Paul is only beginning; his fundamental ideas, disengaged from the elaborate misconceptions with which Protestantism has overlaid them, will have an influence in the future greater than any which they have yet had,—an influence proportioned to their correspondence with a number of the deepest and most permanent facts of human nature itself.

Elsewhere [1] I have pointed out how, for us in this country, Puritanism is the strong and special representative of Protestantism. The Church of England existed before Protestantism, and contains much besides Protestantism. Remove the schemes of doctrine, Calvinistic or Arminian, which for Protestantism, merely as such, have made the very substance of its religion, and all that is most valuable in the Church of England would still remain. These schemes, or the ideas out of which they spring, show themselves in the Prayer Book; but they are not what gives the Prayer Book its importance and value. But Puritanism exists for the sake of these schemes; its organisations are inventions for enforcing them more purely and thoroughly. Questions of discipline and ceremonies have, originally at least, been always admitted to be in themselves secondary; it is because that conception of the ways of God to man which Puritanism has formed for itself appeared to Puritanism superlatively true and precious, that Independents and Baptists and Methodists in England, and Presbyterians in Scotland, have been impelled to constitute for inculcating it a church-order where it might be less swamped by the additions and ceremonies of men, might be more simply and effectively enounced, and might stand more absolute

[1] See *Culture and Anarchy*, chap. iv.

and central, than in the church-order of Anglicans or Roman Catholics.

Of that conception the cardinal points are fixed by the terms *election* and *justification*. These terms come from the writings of St. Paul, and the scheme which Puritanism has constructed with them professes to be St. Paul's scheme. The same or a similar scheme, I repeat, has been, and still is, embraced by many adherents of the Churches of England and Rome ; but these Churches rest their claims to men's interest and attachment not on the possession of such a scheme, but on other grounds with which we have for the present nothing to do. Puritanism's very reason for existing depends on the worth of this its vital conception, derived from St. Paul's writings ; and when we are told that St. Paul is a Protestant doctor whose reign is ending, a Puritan, keen, pugnacious, and sophisticating simple religion of the heart into complicated theories of the brain about election and justification, we in England, at any rate, can best try the assertion by fixing our eyes on our own Puritans, and comparing their doctrine and their hold on vital truth with St. Paul's.

This we propose now to do, and, indeed, to do it will only be to complete what we have already begun. For already, when we were speaking of Hebraism and Hellenism,[1] we were led to remark how the over-Hebraising of Puritanism, and its want of a wide culture, do so narrow its range and impair its vision that even the documents which it thinks all-sufficient, and to the study of which it exclusively rivets itself, it does not rightly understand, but is apt to make of them something quite different from what they really are. In short, no man, we said, who knows nothing else, knows even his Bible. And we showed how readers of the Bible attached to essential words and ideas of the

[1] See *Culture and Anarchy*, chap. v.

Bible a sense which was not the writer's; and in particular how this had happened with regard to the Pauline doctrine of resurrection. Let us take the present opportunity of going further in the same road; and instead of lightly disparaging the great name of St. Paul, let us see if the needful thing is not rather to rescue St. Paul and the Bible from the perversions of them by mistaken men.

So long as the well-known habit, on which we have so often enlarged, prevails amongst our countrymen, of holding mechanically their ideas themselves, but making it their chief aim to work with energy and enthusiasm for the organisations which profess those ideas, English Puritanism is not likely to make such a return upon its own thoughts, and upon the elements of its being, as to accomplish for itself an operation of the kind needed; though it has men whose natural faculties, were they but free to use them, would undoubtedly prove equal to the task. The same habit prevents our Puritans from being reached by philosophical works, which exist in sufficient numbers and of which M. Reuss's history of the growth of Christian theology [1] is an admirable specimen,—works where the entire scheme of Pauline doctrine is laid out with careful research and impartial accuracy. To exhibit the predominant points in Paul's teaching in so plain and popular a manner as to invite and almost compel men's comprehension is not the design of such works; and only by writings with this design in view will English Puritanism be reached.

If when the ideas of St. Paul are so exhibited we are shown that we ought in real truth neither to abase St. Paul and Puritanism together, as M. Renan does, nor to abase St. Paul but exalt Puritanism, nor yet to exalt both Puritan-

---

[1] *Histoire de la Théologie Chrétienne au Siècle Apostolique*, par Edouard Reuss; Strasbourg et Paris (in 2 vols. 8vo.) There is an English translation of M. Reuss's work.

ism and St. Paul together, but rather to abase Puritanism and exalt St. Paul, surely it is best even for Puritanism itself to come to know this. Puritanism certainly wishes well to St. Paul; it cannot wish to compromise him by an unintelligent adhesion to him and a blind adoption of his words, instead of being a true child to him. Yet this is what it has really done. What in St. Paul is secondary and subordinate, Puritanism has made primary and essential; what in St. Paul is figure and belongs to the sphere of feeling, Puritanism has transported into the sphere of intellect and made thesis and formula. On the other hand, what is with St. Paul primary, Puritanism has treated as subordinate: and what is with him thesis and belonging (so far as anything in religion can properly be said thus to belong) to the sphere of intellect, Puritanism has made image and figure.

And first let us premise what we mean in this matter by primary and secondary, essential and subordinate. We mean, so far as the apostle is concerned, a greater or less approach to what really characterises him and gives his teaching its originality and power. We mean, so far as truth is concerned, a greater or less agreement with facts which can be verified, and a greater or less power of explaining them. What essentially characterises a religious teacher, and gives him his permanent worth and vitality, is, after all, just the scientific value of his teaching, its correspondence with important facts and the light it throws on them. Never was the truth of this so evident as now. The scientific sense in man never asserted its claim so strongly; the propensity of religion to neglect those claims, and the peril and loss to it from neglecting them, never were so manifest. The licence of affirmation about God and his proceedings, in which the religious world indulge, is more and more met by the demand for verification. When Calvinism tells us: 'It is agreed between God and the

Mediator Jesus Christ, the Son of God, surety for the redeemed, as parties-contractors, that the sins of the redeemed should be imputed to innocent Christ, and he both condemned and put to death for them, upon this very condition, that whosoever heartily consents unto the covenant of reconciliation offered through Christ, shall, by the imputation of his obedience unto them, be justified and holden righteous before God ;'—when Calvinism tells us this, is it not talking about God just as if he were a man in the next street, whose proceedings Calvinism intimately knew and could give account of, could verify that account at any moment and enable us to verify it also ? It is true, when the scientific sense in us, the sense which seeks exact knowledge, calls for that verification, Calvinism refers us to St. Paul, from whom it professes to have got this history of what it calls 'the covenant of redemption.' But this is only pushing the difficulty a stage further back. For if it is St. Paul, and not Calvinism, that professes this exact acquaintance with God and his doings, the scientific sense calls upon St. Paul to produce the facts by which he verifies what he says; and if he cannot produce them, then it treats both St. Paul's assertion, and Calvinism's assertion after him, as of no real consequence.

No one will deny that such is the behaviour of science towards religion in our day, though many may deplore it. And it is not that the scientific sense in us denies the rights of the poetic sense, which employs a figured and imaginative language. But the language we have just been quoting is not figurative and poetic language, it is scholastic and scientific language. Assertions in scientific language must stand the tests of scientific examination. Neither is it that the scientific sense in us refuses to admit willingly and reverently the name of God, as a point in which the religious and the scientific sense may meet, as the least inadequate name for that universal order which the intellect feels after as a law and the heart feels after as a benefit. 'We, too,' might the men of science say to the men of religion,—'we, too, would gladly say *God*, if only, the moment one says *God*, you would not pester one with your pretensions of knowing all about him.' That *stream of tendency by which all things seek to fulfil the law of their being*, and which, inasmuch as our idea of real welfare resolves itself into this fulfilment of the law of one's being, man rightly deems the fountain of all goodness, and calls by the worthiest and most solemn name he can, which is God, science also might willingly own for the fountain of all goodness, and call God. But however much more than this the heart may with propriety put into its language respecting God, this is as much as science can with strictness put there. Therefore when the religious world, following its bent of trying to describe what it loves, amplifying and again amplifying its description, and guarding finally this amplified description by the most precise and rigid terms it can find, comes at last, with the best intentions, to the notion of a sort of magnified and non-natural man, who proceeds in the fashion laid down in the Calvinistic thesis we have quoted, then science strikes in, remarks the difference between this second notion and the notion it originally admitted, and demands to have the new notion verified, as the first can be verified, by facts. But this does not unsettle the first notion, or prevent science from acknowledging the importance and the scientific validity of propositions which are grounded upon the first notion and shed light over it.

Nevertheless, researches in this sphere are now a good deal eclipsed in popularity by researches in the sphere of physics, and no longer have the vogue which they once had. I have related how an eminent physicist with whose acquaintance I am honoured imagines me to have invented the author of the *Sacra Privata*; and that fashionable newspaper, the *Morning Post*, undertaking,—as I seemed, it said, very anxious about the matter,—to supply information as to who the author really was, laid it down that he was Bishop of Calcutta, and that his ideas and writings, to which I attached so much value, had been among the main provocatives of the Indian mutiny. Therefore it is perhaps expedient to refresh our memory as to these schemes of doctrine, Calvinistic or Arminian, to uphold which, as has been said, British Puritanism exists, before we proceed to compare them, for correspondence with facts and for scientific validity, with the teaching of St. Paul.

Calvinism, then, begins by laying down that God from all eternity decreed whatever was to come to pass in time; that by his decree a certain number of angels and men are predestinated, out of God's mere free grace and love, without any foresight of faith or good works in them, to everlasting life; and others foreordained, according to the unsearchable counsel of his will, whereby he extends or withholds mercy as he pleases, to everlasting death. God made, however, our first parents, Adam and Eve, upright and able to keep his law, which was written in their hearts; at the same time entering into a contract with them, and with their posterity as represented in them, by which they were assured of everlasting life in return for perfect obedience, and of everlasting death if they should be disobedient. Our first parents, being enticed by Satan, a fallen angel speaking in the form of a serpent, broke this *covenant of works*, as it is called, by eating the forbidden fruit; and hereby they, and their posterity in them and with them, became not only liable to eternal death, but lost also their natural uprightness and all ability to please God; nay, they became by nature enemies to God and to all spiritual good, and inclined only to evil continually. This, says Calvinism, is our original sin; the bitter root of all our actual transgressions, in thought, word, and deed.

Yet, though man has neither power nor inclination to rise out of this wretched fallen state, but is rather disposed to lie insensible in it till he perish, another covenant exists by which his condition is greatly affected. This is the *covenant of redemption*, made and agreed upon, says Calvinism, between God the Father and God the Son in the Council of the Trinity before the world began. The sum of the covenant of redemption is this: God having, by the eternal decree already mentioned, freely chosen to life a certain number of lost mankind, gave them before the world began to God the Son, appointed Redeemer on condition that if he humbled himself so far as to assume the human nature in union with the divine nature, submit himself to the law as surety for the elect, and satisfy justice for them by giving obedience in their name, even to suffering the cursed death of the cross, he should ransom and redeem them from sin and death, and purchase for them righteousness and eternal life. The Son of God accepted the condition, or *bargain*, as Calvinism calls it; and in the fulness of time came, as Jesus Christ, into the world, was born of the Virgin Mary, subjected himself to the law, and completely paid the due ransom on the cross.

God has in his word, the Bible, revealed to man this covenant of grace or redemption. All those whom he has predestinated to life he in his own time effectually calls to be partakers in the release offered. Man is altogether passive in this call, until the Holy Spirit enables him to answer it. The Holy Spirit, the third person in the Trinity, applies to the elect the redemption purchased by Christ, through working faith in them. As soon as the elect have faith in Jesus Christ, that is, as soon as they give their consent heartily and repentantly, in the sense of deserved condemnation, to the covenant of grace, God justifies them by imputing to them that perfect obedience which Christ gave to the law, and the satisfaction also which upon the cross Christ gave to justice in their name. They who are thus called and justified are by the same power likewise sanctified; the dominion of carnal lusts being destroyed in them, and the practice of holiness being, in spite of some remnants of corruption, put in their power. Good works, done in obedience to God's moral law, are the fruits and evidences of a true faith; and the persons of the faithful elect being accepted through Christ, their good works also are accepted in him and rewarded. But works done by other and unregenerate men, though they may be things which God commands, cannot please God and are sinful. The elect can after justification and sanctification no more fall from the state of grace, but shall certainly persevere to the end and be eternally saved; and of this they may, even in the present life, have the certain assurance. Finally, after death, their souls and bodies are joyfully joined together again in the resurrection, and they remain thenceforth for ever with Christ in glory; while all the wicked are sent away into hell with Satan, whom they have served.

We have here set down the main doctrines of Calvinistic Puritanism almost entirely in formal words of its own choosing. It is not necessary to enter into distinctions such as those between sublapsarians and supralapsarians, between Calvinists who believe that God's decree of election and reprobation was passed in foresight of original sin and on account of it, and Calvinists who believe that it was passed absolutely and independently. The important points of Calvinism,—original sin, free election, effectual calling, justification through imputed righteousness,—are common to both. The passiveness of man, the activity of God, are the great features in this scheme; there is very little of what man thinks and does, very much of what God thinks and does; and what God thinks and does is described with such particularity that the figure I have used of the man in the next street cannot but recur strongly to our minds.

The positive Protestantism of Puritanism, with which we are here concerned, as distinguished from the negative Protestantism of the Church of England, has nourished itself with ardour on this scheme of doctrine. It informs and fashions the whole religion of Scotland, established and nonconforming. It is the doctrine which Puritan flocks delight to hear from their pastors. It was Puritanism's constant reproach against the Church of England, that this essential doctrine was not firmly enough held and set forth by her. At the Hampton Court Conference in 1604, in the Committee of Divines appointed by the House of Lords in 1641, and again at the Savoy Conference in 1661, the reproach regularly appeared. 'Some have defended,' is the Puritan complaint, 'the whole gross substance of Arminianism, that the act of conversion depends upon the concurrence of man's free will; some do teach and preach that good works are concauses with faith in the act of justification; some have defended universal grace, some have absolutely denied original sin.' As Puritanism grew, the Calvinistic scheme of doctrine hardened and became stricter. Of the Calvinistic confessions of faith of the sixteenth century,—the Helvetic Confession, the Belgic Confession, the Heidelberg Catechism,—the Calvinism is so moderate as to astonish any one who has been used only to its later developments. Even the much-abused canons of the Synod of Dort no one can read through attentively without finding in parts of them a genuine movement of thought,—sometimes even a philosophic depth,—and a powerful religious feeling. In the documents of the Westminster Assembly, twenty-five years later, this has disappeared; and what we call the British

Philistine stands in his religious capacity, sheer and stark, before us. Seriousness is the one merit of these documents, but it is a seriousness too mixed with the alloy of mundane strife and hatred to be called a religious feeling. Not a trace of delicacy of perception, or of philosophic thinking; the mere rigidness and contentiousness of the controversialist and political dissenter; a Calvinism exaggerated till it is simply repelling; and to complete the whole, a machinery of covenants, conditions, bargains, and parties-contractors, such as could have proceeded from no one but the born Anglo-Saxon man of business, British or American.

However, a scheme of doctrine is not necessarily false because of the style in which its adherents may have at a particular moment enounced it. From the faults which disfigure the performance of the Westminster divines the profession of faith prefixed to the Congregational *Year-Book* is free. The Congregationalists form one of the two great divisions of English Puritans. 'Congregational churches believe,' their *Year-Book* tells us, 'that the first man disobeyed the divine command, fell from his state of innocence and purity, and involved all his posterity in the consequences of that fall. They believe that all who will be saved were the objects of God's eternal and electing love, and were given by an act of divine sovereignty to the Son of God. They believe that Christ meritoriously obtained eternal redemption for us, and that the Holy Spirit is given in consequence of Christ's Mediation.' The essential points of Calvinism are all here. To this profession of faith, published in the *Year-Book* of the Independents, subscription is not required; Puritanism thus remaining honourably consistent with the protests which, at the Restoration, it made against the call for subscription. But the authors of the *Year-Book* say with pride, and it is a common boast of the Independent churches, that though they do not require subscription, there is, perhaps, in no religious body, such firm and general agreement in doctrine as among Congregationalists. This is true, and it is even more true of the flocks than of the ministers, of whom the abler and the younger begin to be lifted by the stream of modern ideas. Still, up to the present time, the Protestantism of one great division of English Puritans is undoubtedly Calvinist; the Baptists holding in general the scheme of Calvinism yet more strictly than the Independents.

The other great division of English Puritanism is formed by the Methodists. Wesleyan Methodism is, as is well known, not Calvinist, but Arminian. The *Methodist Magazine* was called by Wesley the *Arminian Magazine*, and kept that title all through his life. Arminianism is an attempt made with the best intentions, and with much truth of practical sense, but not in a very profound philosophical spirit, to escape from what perplexes and shocks in Calvinism. The God of Calvinism is a magnified and non-natural man who decrees at his mere good pleasure some men to salvation and other men to reprobation; the God of Arminianism is a magnified and non-natural man who foreknows the course of each man's life, and who decrees each of us to salvation or reprobation in accordance with this foreknowledge. But so long as we remain in this anthropomorphic order of ideas the question will always occur: Why did not a being of infinite power and infinite love so make all men as that there should be no cause for this sad foreknowledge and sad decree respecting a number of them? In truth, Calvinism is both theologically more coherent, and also shows a deeper sense of reality than Arminianism, which, in the practical man's fashion, is apt to scrape the surface of things only.

For instance, the Arminian Remonstrants, in their zeal

to justify the morality, in a human sense, of God's ways, maintained that he sent his word to one nation rather than another according as he saw that one nation was more worthy than another of such a preference. The Calvinist doctors of the Synod of Dort have no difficulty in showing that Moses and Christ both of them assert, with respect to the Jewish nation, the direct contrary; and not only do they here obtain a theological triumph, but in rebutting the Arminian theory they are in accordance with historical truth and with the real march of human affairs. They allow more for the great fact of the *not ourselves* in what we do and are. The Calvinists seize, we say, that great fact better than the Arminians. The Calvinist's fault is in his scientific appreciation of the fact; in the reasons he gives for it. God, he says, sends his word to one nation rather than another *at his mere good pleasure.* Here we have again the magnified and non-natural man, who likes and dislikes, knows and decrees, just as a man, only on a scale immensely transcending anything of which we have experience; and whose proceedings we nevertheless describe as if he were in the next street for people to verify all we say about him.

Arminian Methodism, however, puts aside the Calvinistic doctrine of predestination. The foremost place, which in the Calvinist scheme belongs to the doctrine of predestination, belongs in the Methodist scheme to the doctrine of justification by faith. More and more prominently does modern Methodism elevate this as its essential doctrine; and the era in their founder's life which Methodists select to celebrate is the era of his conversion to it. It is the doctrine of Anselm, adopted and developed by Luther, set forth in the Confession of Augsburg, and current all through the popular theology of our day. We shall find it in almost any popular hymn we happen to take, but the following lines of Milton exhibit it classically. By the fall of our first parents, says he :—

> Man, losing all,
> To expiate his treason hath nought left,
> But to destruction sacred and devote
> He with his whole posterity must die;
> Die he or justice must; unless for him
> Some other able, and as willing, pay
> The rigid satisfaction; death for death.

By Adam's fall, God's justice and mercy were placed in conflict. God could not follow his mercy without violating his justice. Christ by his satisfaction gave the Father the right and power (*nudum jus Patri acquirebat*, said the Arminians) to follow his mercy, and to make with man the covenant of free justification by faith, whereby, if a man has a sure trust and confidence that his sins are forgiven him in virtue of the satisfaction made to God for them by the death of Christ, he is held clear of sin by God and admitted to salvation.

This doctrine, like the Calvinist doctrine of predestination, involves a whole history of God's proceedings, and gives, also, first and almost sole place to what God does, with disregard to what man does. It has thus an essential affinity with Calvinism; indeed, Calvinism is but this doctrine of original sin and justification, *plus* the doctrine of predestination. Nay, the Welsh Methodists, as is well known, have no difficulty in combining the tenet of election with the practices and most of the tenets of Methodism. The word *solifidian* points precisely to that which is common to both Calvinism and Methodism, and which has made both these halves of English Puritanism so popular,—their *sensational* side, as it may be called, their laying all stress on a wonderful and particular account of what God gives and works for us, not on what we bring or do for ourselves.

'Plead thou singly,' says Wesley, 'the blood of the covenant, the ransom paid for thy proud stubborn soul.' Wesley's doctrines of conversion, of the new birth, of sanctification, of the direct witness of the spirit, of assurance, of sinless perfection, all of them thus correspond with doctrines which we have noticed in Calvinism, and show a common character with them. The instantaneousness Wesley loved to ascribe to conversion and sanctification points the same way. 'God gives in a moment such a faith in the blood of his Son as translates us out of darkness into light, out of sin and fear into holiness and happiness.' And again, 'Look for sanctification just as you are, as a poor sinner that has nothing to pay, nothing to plead but *Christ died.*' This is the side in Wesley's teaching which his followers have above all seized, and which they are eager to hold forth as the essential part of his legacy towards them.

It is true that from the same reason which prevents, as we have said, those who know their Bible and nothing else from really knowing even their Bible, Methodists, who for the most part know nothing but Wesley, do not really know even Wesley. It is true that what really characterises this most interesting and most attractive man, is not his doctrine of justification by faith, or any other of his set doctrines, but is entirely what we may call his *genius for godliness.* Mr. Alexander Knox, in his remarks on his friend's life and character, insists much on an entry in Wesley's Journal in 1767, where he seems impatient at the endless harping on the tenet of justification, and where he asks 'if it is not high time to return to the plain word : " He that feareth God and worketh righteousness is accepted with him."' Mr. Knox is right in thinking that the feeling which made Wesley ask this is what gave him his vital worth and character as a man ; but it is not what gives him his character as the teacher of Methodism. Methodism rejects Mr. Knox's version of its founder, and insists on making the article of justification the very corner-stone of the Wesleyan edifice.

And the truth undoubtedly is, that not by his assertion of what man brings, but by his assertion of what God gives, by his doctrines of conversion, instantaneous justification and sanctification, assurance and sinless perfection, does Wesley live and operate in Methodism. 'You think, I must first be or do thus or thus (for sanctification). Then you are seeking it by works unto this day. If you seek it by faith, you may expect it as you are; then expect it now. It is of importance to observe that there is an inseparable connexion between these three points : expect it *by faith*, expect it *as you are*, and expect it *now*. To deny one of them is to deny them all; to allow one is to allow them all.' This is the teaching of Wesley which has made the great Methodist half of English Puritanism what it is, and not his hesitations and recoils at the dangers of his own teaching.

No doubt, as the seriousness of Calvinism, its perpetual conversance with deep matters and with the Bible, have given force and fervency to Calvinist Puritans, so the loveliness of Wesley's piety, and what I have called his genius for godliness, have sweetened and made amiable numberless lives of Methodist Puritans. But as a religious teacher, Wesley is to be judged by his doctrine; and his doctrine, like the Calvinistic scheme, rests with all its weight on the assertion of certain minutely described proceedings on God's part, independent of us, our experience, and our will; and leads its recipients to look, in religion, not so much for an arduous progress on their own part, and the exercise of their activity, as for strokes of magic, and what may be called a sensational character.

In the Heidelberg Catechism, after an answer in which the catechist rehearses the popularly received doctrine of original sin and vicarious satisfaction for it, the catechiser asks the pertinent question : '*Unde id scis?*'—how do you know all that? The Apostle Paul is, as we have already shown, the great authority for it whom formal theology invokes; his name is used by popular theology with the same confidence. I open a modern book of popular religion at the account of a visit paid to a hardened criminal seized with terror the night before his execution. The visitor addresses him : '*I now stand in Paul's place*, and say : In Christ's stead we pray you, be ye reconciled to God. I beg you to accept the pardon of all your sins, which Christ has purchased for you, and which God freely bestows on you for his sake. If you do not understand, I say : God's ways are not as our ways.' And the narrative of the criminal's conversion goes on : 'That night was spent in singing the praises of the Saviour who had purchased his pardon.'

Both Calvinism and Methodism appeal, therefore, to the Bible, and, above all, to St. Paul, for the history they propound of the relations between God and man ; but Calvinism relies most, in enforcing it, on man's fears, Methodism on man's hopes. Calvinism insists on man's being under a curse ; it then works the sense of sin, misery, and terror in him, and appeals pre-eminently to the desire to flee from the wrath to come. Methodism, too, insists on his being under a curse ; but it works most the sense of hope in him, the craving for happiness, and appeals pre-eminently to the desire for eternal bliss. No one, however, will maintain that the particular account of God's proceedings with man, whereby Methodism and Calvinism operate on these desires, proves itself by internal evidence, and establishes without external aid its own scientific validity. So we may either directly try, as best we can, its scientific validity in itself; or, as it professes to have Paul's authority to support it, we may first inquire what is really Paul's account of

God's proceedings with man, and whether this tallies with the Puritan account and confirms it. The latter is in every way the safer and the more instructive course to follow. And we will follow Puritanism's example in taking St. Paul's mature and greatest work, the Epistle to the Romans, as the chief place for finding what he really thought on the points in question.

We have already said elsewhere,[1] indeed, what is very true, and what must never be forgotten, that what St. Paul, a man so separated from us by time, race, training and circumstances, really thought, we cannot make sure of knowing exactly. All we can do is to get near it, reading him with the sort of critical tact which the study of the human mind and its history, and the acquaintance with many great writers, naturally gives for following the movement of any one single great writer's thought; reading him, also, without preconceived theories to which we want to make his thoughts fit themselves. It is evident that the English translation of the Epistle to the Romans has been made by men with their heads full of the current doctrines of election and justification we have been noticing; and it has thereby received such a bias,—of which a strong example is the use of the word *atonement* in the eleventh verse of the fifth chapter,—that perhaps it is almost impossible for any one who reads the English translation only, to take into his mind Paul's thought without a colouring from the current doctrines. But besides discarding the English translation, we must bear in mind, if we wish to get as near Paul's real thought as possible, two things which have greatly increased the facilities for misrepresenting him.

In the first place, Paul, like the other Bible-writers, and like the Semitic race in general, has a much juster sense of the true scope and limits of diction in religious deliverances

[1] See *Culture and Anarchy*, chap. v.

than we have. He uses within the sphere of religious emotion expressions which, in this sphere, have an eloquence and a propriety, but which are not to be taken out of it and made into formal scientific propositions.

This is a point very necessary to be borne in mind in reading the Bible. The prophet Nahum says in the book of his vision: '*God is jealous, and the Lord revengeth;*'[1] and the authors of the Westminster Confession, drawing out a scientific theology, lay down the proposition that God is a jealous and vengeful God, and think they prove their proposition by quoting in a note the words of Nahum. But this is as if we took from a chorus of Æschylus one of his grand passages about guilt and destiny, just put the words straight into the formal and exact cast of a sentence of Aristotle, and said that here was the scientific teaching of Greek philosophy on these matters. The Hebrew genius has not, like the Greek, its conscious and clear-marked division into a poetic side and a scientific side; the scientific side is almost absent. The Bible utterances have often the character of a chorus of Æschylus, but never that of a treatise of Aristotle. We, like the Greeks, possess in our speech and thought the two characters; but so far as the Bible is concerned we have generally confounded them, and have used our double possession for our bewilderment rather than turned it to good account. The admirable maxim of the great mediæval Jewish school of Biblical critics: *The Law speaks with the tongue of the children of men,*—a maxim which is the very foundation of all sane Biblical criticism,—was for centuries a dead letter to the whole body of our Western exegesis, and is a dead letter to the whole body of our popular exegesis still. Taking the Bible language as equivalent with the language of the scientific intellect, a language which is adequate and absolute,

[1] Nahum, i, 2.

we have never been in a position to use the key which this maxim of the Jewish doctors offers to us. But it is certain that, whatever strain the religious expressions of the Semitic genius were meant, in the minds of those who gave utterance to them, to bear, the particular strain which we Western people put upon them is one which they were not meant to bear.

I have used the word *Hebraise*[1] for another purpose,— to denote the exclusive attention to the moral side of our nature, to conscience, and to doing rather than knowing; so, to describe the vivid and figured way in which St. Paul within the sphere of religious emotion uses words without carrying them outside it, I will use the word *Orientalise*. When Paul says: 'God hath concluded them all in unbelief *that he might* have mercy upon all,' he Orientalises; that is, he does not mean to assert formally that God acted with this set design, but, being full of the happy and divine end to the unbelief spoken of, he, by a vivid and striking figure, represents the unbelief as actually caused with a view to this end. But when the Calvinists of the Synod of Dort, wishing to establish the formal proposition that faith and all saving gifts flow from election and nothing else, quote an expression of Paul's similar to the one we have quoted, 'He hath chosen us,' they say, 'not because we were, but *that we might be* holy and without blame before him,'[2] they go quite wide of the mark, from not perceiving that what the apostle used as a vivid figure of rhetoric, they are using as a formal scientific proposition.

When Paul Orientalises, the fault is not with him if he is misunderstood, but with the prosaic and unintelligent Western readers who have not enough tact for style to comprehend his mode of expression. But he also Judaises; and here his liability to being misunderstood by us Western

[1] See *Culture and Anarchy*, chap. iv.   [2] *Rom.*, xi, 32.

people is undoubtedly due to a defect in the critical habit of himself and his race. A Jew himself, he uses the Jewish Scriptures in a Jew's arbitrary and uncritical fashion, as if they had a talismanic character ; as if for a doctrine, however true in itself, their confirmation was still necessary, and as if this confirmation was to be got from their mere words alone, however detached from the sense of their context, and however violently allegorised or otherwise wrested.

To use the Bible in this way, even for purposes of illustration, is often an interruption to the argument, a fault of style ; to use it in this way for real proof and confirmation, is a fault of reasoning. An example of the first fault may be seen in the tenth chapter of the Epistle to the Romans, and in the beginning of the third chapter. The apostle's point in either place,—his point that faith comes by hearing, and his point that God's oracles were true though the Jews did not believe them,—would stand much clearer without their scaffolding of Bible-quotation. An instance of the second fault is in the third and fourth chapters of the Epistle to the Galatians, where the Biblical argumentation by which the apostle seeks to prove his case is as unsound as his case itself is sound. How far these faults are due to the apostle himself, how far to the requirements of those for whom he wrote, we need not now investigate. It is enough that he undoubtedly uses the letter of Scripture in this arbitrary and Jewish way ; and thus Puritanism, which has only itself to blame for misunderstanding him when he Orientalises, may fairly put upon the apostle himself some of its blame for misunderstanding him when he Judaises, and for Judaising so strenuously along with him.

To get, therefore, at what Paul really thought and meant to say, it is necessary for us modern and Western people to translate him. And not as Puritanism, which has merely taken his letter and re-set it in the formal propositions of a modern scientific treatise; but his letter itself must be recast before it can be properly conveyed by such propositions. And as the order in which, in any series of ideas, the ideas come, is of great importance to the final result, and as Paul, who did not write scientific treatises, but had always religious edification in direct view, never set out his doctrine with a design of exhibiting it as a scientific whole, we must also find out for ourselves the order in which Paul's ideas naturally stand, and the connexion between one of them and the other, in order to arrive at the real scheme of his teaching, as compared with the schemes exhibited by Puritanism.

We remarked how what sets the Calvinist in motion seems to be the desire to flee from the wrath to come; and what sets the Methodist in motion, the desire for eternal bliss. What is it which sets Paul in motion? It is the impulse which we have elsewhere noted as the master-impulse of Hebraism,—*the desire for righteousness*. 'I exercise myself,' he told Felix, '*to have a conscience void of offence towards God and men continually.*'[1] To the Hebrew, this moral order, or righteousness, was pre-eminently the universal order, the law of God; and God, the fountain of all goodness, was pre-eminently to him the giver of the moral law. The end and aim of all religion, *access to God*,—the sense of harmony with the universal order, the partaking of the divine nature, that our faith and hope might be in God, that we might have life and have it more abundantly,— meant for the Hebrew, access to the source of the *moral* order in especial, and harmony with it. It was the greatness of the Hebrew race that it felt the authority of this order, its preciousness and its beneficence, so strongly. 'How precious are thy thoughts unto me, O God!'—'The law of thy mouth is better than thousands of gold and silver.'— 'My soul is consumed with the very fervent desire that it

[1] *Acts*, xxiv, 16.

hath alway unto thy judgments.'[1] It was the greatness of their best individuals that in them this feeling was incessantly urgent to prove itself in the only sure manner,—in action. 'Blessed are they who hear the word of God, and *keep* it.' 'If thou wouldst enter into life, *keep* the commandments.' 'Let no man deceive you, he that *doeth* righteousness is righteous.'[2] What distinguishes Paul is both his conviction that the commandment is holy, and just, and good; and also his desire to give effect to the commandment, to *establish* it. It was this which gave to his endeavour after a clear conscience such meaning and efficacy. It was this which gave him insight to see that there could be no radical difference, in respect of salvation and the way to it, between Jew and Gentile. 'Upon every soul of man that *worketh evil*, whoever he may be, tribulation and anguish; to every one that *worketh good*, glory, honour, and peace!'[3]

St. Paul's piercing practical religious sense, joined to his strong intellectual power, enabled him to discern and follow the range of the commandment, both as to man's actions and as to his heart and thoughts, with extraordinary force and closeness. His religion had, as we shall see, a preponderantly mystic side, and nothing is so natural to the mystic as in rich single words, such as *faith, light, love*, to sum up and take for granted, without specially enumerating them, all good moral principles and habits; yet nothing is more remarkable in Paul than the frequent, nay, incessant lists, in the most particular detail, of moral habits to be pursued or avoided. Lists of this sort might in a less sincere and profound writer be formal and wearisome; but to no attentive reader of St. Paul will they be wearisome, for in making them he touched the solid ground which was the basis of his

[1] *Ps.* cxxxix, 7; cxix, 72; *Ibid.*, 20.
[2] Luke, xi, 28; Matth., xix, 17; 1 John, iii, 7.
[3] *Rom.*, ii, 9, 10.

religion,—the solid ground of his hearty desire for righteousness and of his thorough conception of it,—and only on such a ground was so strong a superstructure possible. The more one studies these lists, the more does their significance come out. To illustrate this, let any one go through for himself the enumeration, too long to be quoted here, in the four last verses of the first chapter of the Epistle to the Romans, of 'things which are not convenient;' or let him merely consider with attention this catalogue, towards the end of the fifth chapter of the Epistle to the Galatians, of fruits of the spirit: 'love, joy, peace, patience, kindness, goodness, faith, mildness, self-control.'[1] The man who wrote with this searching minuteness knew accurately what he meant by sin and righteousness, and did not use these words at random. His diligent comprehensiveness in his plan of duties is only less admirable than his diligent sincerity. The sterner virtues and the gentler, his conscience will not let him rest till he has embraced them all. In his deep resolve 'to make out by actual trial what is that good and perfect and acceptable will of God,'[2] he goes back upon himself again and again, he marks a duty at every point of our nature, and at points the most opposite, for fear he should by possibility be leaving behind him some weakness still indulged, some subtle promptings to evil not yet brought into captivity.

It has not been enough remarked how this incomparable honesty and depth in Paul's love of righteousness is probably what chiefly explains his conversion. Most men have the defects, as the saying is, of their qualities. Because they are ardent and severe they have no sense for gentleness and sweetness; because they are sweet and gentle they have no sense for severity and ardour. A Puritan is a Puritan, and a man of feeling is a man of feeling. But with Paul the

[1] Verses 22, 23. [2] *Rom.*, xii, 2.

very same fulness of moral nature which made him an ardent Pharisee, 'as concerning zeal, persecuting the church, touching the righteousness which is in the law, blameless,' was so large that it carried him out of Pharisaism and beyond it, when once he found how much needed doing in him which Pharisaism could not do.

Every attentive regarder of the character of Paul, not only as he was before his conversion but as he appears to us till his end, must have been struck with two things: one, the earnest insistence with which he recommends 'bowels of mercies,' as he calls them; meekness, humbleness of mind, gentleness, unwearying forbearance, crowned all of them with that emotion of charity 'which is the bond of perfectness;' the other, the force with which he dwells on the *solidarity* (to use the modern phrase) of mankind,—the joint interest, that is, which binds humanity together,—the duty of respecting every one's part in life, and of doing justice to his efforts to fulfil that part. Never surely did such a controversialist, such a master of sarcasm and invective, commend, with such manifest sincerity and such persuasive emotion, the qualities of meekness and gentleness! Never surely did a worker who took with such energy his own line, and who was so born to preponderate and predominate in whatever line he took, insist so often and so admirably that the lines of other workers were just as good as his own! At no time, perhaps, did Paul arrive at practising quite perfectly what he thus preached; but this only sets in a stronger light the thorough love of righteousness which made him seek out, and put so prominently forward, and so strive to make himself and others fulfil, parts of righteousness which do not force themselves on the common conscience like the duties of soberness, temperance, and activity, and which were somewhat alien, certainly, to his own particular nature. Therefore we cannot but believe that into this spirit, so possessed with the hunger and thirst for righteousness, and precisely because it was so possessed by it, the characteristic doctrines of Jesus, which brought a new aliment to feed this hunger and thirst,—of Jesus whom, except in vision, he had never seen, but who was in every one's words and thoughts, the teacher who was mild and lowly in heart, who said men were brothers and must love one another, that the last should often be first, that the exercise of dominion and lordship had nothing in them desirable, and that we must become as little children,—sank down and worked there even before Paul ceased to persecute, and had no small part in getting him ready for the crisis of his conversion.

Such doctrines offered new fields of righteousness to the eye of this indefatigable explorer of it, and enlarged the domain of duty of which Pharisaism showed him only a portion. Then, after the satisfaction thus given to his desire for a full conception of righteousness, came Christ's injunctions to make clean the inside as well as the outside, to beware of the least leaven of hypocrisy and self-flattery, of saying and not doing;—and, finally, the injunction to feel, after doing all we can, that, as compared with the standard of perfection, we are still unprofitable servants. These teachings were, to a man like Paul, for the practice of righteousness what the others were for the theory;—sympathetic utterances, which made the inmost chords of his being vibrate, and which irresistibly drew him sooner or later towards their utterer. Need it be said that he never forgot them, and that in all his pages they have left their trace? It is even affecting to see, how, when he is driven for the very sake of righteousness to put the law of righteousness in the second place, and to seek outside the law itself for a power to fulfil the law, how, I say, he returns again and again to the elucidation of his one sole design in all he is doing; how he labours to prevent all possibility of misunderstanding, and to show that he is only leaving the moral law for a moment in order to establish it for ever more victoriously. What earnestness and pathos in the assurance: 'If there had been a law given which could have given life, verily righteousness should have been by the law!'[1] 'Do I condemn the law?' he keeps saying; 'do I forget that the commandment is holy, just, and good? Because we are no longer under the law, are we to sin? Am I seeking to make the course of my life and yours other than a service and an obedience?' This man, out of whom a blinded criticism has deduced Antinomianism, is in truth so possessed with horror of Antinomianism, that he goes to grace for the sole purpose of extirpating it, and even then cannot rest without perpetually telling us why he is gone there. This man, whom Calvin and Luther and their followers have shut up into the two scholastic doctrines of election and justification, would have said, could we hear him, just what he said about circumcision and uncircumcision in his own day: 'Election is nothing, and justification is nothing, but the keeping of the commandments of God.'

This foremost place which righteousness takes in the order of St. Paul's ideas makes a signal difference between him and Puritanism. Puritanism, as we have said, finds its starting-point either in the desire to flee from eternal wrath or in the desire to obtain eternal bliss. Puritanism has learned from revelation, as it says, a particular history of the first man's fall, of mankind being under a curse, of certain contracts having been passed concerning mankind in the Council of the Trinity, of the substance of those contracts, and of man's position under them. The great concern of Puritanism is with the operation of those contracts on man's condition; its leading thought, if it is a Puritanism of a gloomy turn, is of awe and fear caused by the threatening aspect of man's condition under these contracts; if of a

[1] *Gal.*, iii, 21.

cheerful turn, of gratitude and hope caused by the favourable aspect of it. But in either case, foregone events, the covenant passed, what God has done and does, is the great matter. What there is left for man to do, the human work of righteousness, is secondary, and comes in but to attest and confirm our assurance of what God has done for us. We have seen this in Wesley's words already quoted: the first thing for a man is to be justified and sanctified, and to have the assurance that, without seeking it by works, he is justified and sanctified; then the desire and works of righteousness follow as a proper result of this condition. Still more does Calvinism make man's desire and works of righteousness mere evidences and benefits of more important things; the desire to work righteousness is among the saving graces applied by the Holy Spirit to the elect, and the last of those graces. *Denique*, says the Synod of Dort, *last of all*, after faith in the promises and after the witness of the Spirit, comes, to establish our assurance, a clear conscience and righteousness. It is manifest how unlike is this order of ideas to Paul's order, who starts with the thought of a conscience void of offence towards God and man, and builds upon that thought his whole system.

But this difference constitutes from the very outset an immense scientific superiority for the scheme of Paul. Hope and fear are elements of human nature like the love of right, but they are far blinder and less scientific elements of it. 'The Bible is a divine revelation; the Bible declares certain things; the things it thus declares have the witness of our hopes and fears;'—this is the line of thought followed by Puritanism. But what science seeks after is a satisfying rational conception of things. A scheme which fails to give this, which gives the contrary of this, may indeed be of a nature to move our hopes and fears, but is to science of none the more value on that account.

Nor does our calling such a scheme *a revelation* mend the matter. Instead of covering the scientific inadequacy of a conception by the authority of a revelation, science rather proves the authority of a revelation by the scientific adequacy of the conceptions given in it, and limits the sphere of that authority to the sphere of that adequacy. The more an alleged revelation seems to contain precious and true things, the more ought we to be inclined to doubt the correctness of any deduction which draws from it, within the sphere of these things, a scheme which rationally is not satisfying. That the scheme of Puritanism is rationally so little satisfying should incline us, not to take it on the authority of the Bible, but to doubt whether it is really in the Bible. The first appeal which this scheme, having begun outside the sphere of reality and experience, makes in the sphere of reality and experience,—its first appeal, therefore, to science,—the appeal to the witness of human hope and fear, does not much mend matters ; for science knows that numberless conceptions not rationally satisfying are yet the ground of hope and fear.

Paul does not begin outside the sphere of science ; he begins with an appeal to reality and experience. And the appeal here with which he commences has, for science, undoubted force and importance ; for he appeals to a rational conception which is a part, and perhaps the chief part, of our experience ; the conception of the law of *righteousness*, the very law and ground of human nature so far as this nature is moral. Things as they truly are, facts, are the object-matter of science ; and the moral law in human nature, however this law may have originated, is in our actual experience among the greatest of facts.

If I were not afraid of intruding upon Mr. Ruskin's province, I might point out the witness which etymology itself bears to this law as a prime element and *clue* in man's constitution. Our word righteousness means going straight, going the way we are meant to go; there are languages in which the word 'way' or 'road' is also the word for right reason and duty; the Greek word for justice and righteousness has for its foundation, some say, the idea of describing a certain line, following a certain necessary orbit. But for these fanciful helps there is no need. When Paul starts with affirming the grandeur and necessity of the law of righteousness, science has no difficulty in going along with him. When he fixes as man's right aim 'love, joy, peace, patience, kindness, goodness, faith, mildness, self-control,'[1] he appeals for witness to the truth of what he says to an experience too intimate to need illustration or argument.

The best confirmation of the scientific validity of the importance which Paul thus attaches to the law of righteousness, the law of reason and conscience, God as moral law, is to be found in its agreement with the importance attached to this law by teachers the most unlike him; since in the eye of science an experience gains as much by having universality, as in the eye of religion it seems to gain by having uniqueness. 'Would you know,' says Epictetus, 'the means to perfection which Socrates followed? they were these: in every single matter which came before him he made the rule of reason and conscience his one rule to follow.' Such was precisely the aim of Paul also; it is an aim to which science does homage as a satisfying rational conception. And to this aim hope and fear properly attach themselves. For on our following the clue of moral order, or losing it, depends our happiness or misery; our life or death in the true sense of those words; our harmony with the universal order or our disharmony with it; our partaking, as St. Paul says, of the wrath of God or of the glory of God. So that looking to this clue, and fearing to lose hold on it, we may

[1] *Gal.*, v, 22, 23.

in strict scientific truth say with the author of the Imitation : *Omnia vanitas, præter amare Deum, et illi soli servire.*

But to serve God, to follow that central clue in our moral being which unites us to the universal order, is no easy task ; and here again we are on the most sure ground of experience and psychology. In some way or other, says Bishop Wilson, every man is conscious of an opposition in him between the flesh and the spirit. *Video meliora proboque, deteriora sequor,* say the thousand times quoted lines of the Roman poet. The philosophical explanation of this conflict does not indeed attribute, like the Manichæan fancy, any inherent evil to the flesh and its workings ; all the forces and tendencies in us are, like our proper central moral tendency the desire of righteousness, in themselves beneficent. But they require to be harmonised with this tendency, because this aims directly at our total moral welfare,—our harmony as moral beings with the law of our nature and the law of God,—and derives thence a pre-eminence and a right to moderate. And, though they are not evil in themselves, the evil which flows from these diverse workings is undeniable. The lusts of the flesh, the law in our members, *passion*, according to the Greek word used by Paul, *inordinate affection*, according to the admirable rendering of Paul's Greek word in our English Bible,[1] take naturally no account of anything but themselves ; this arbitrary and unregulated action of theirs can produce only confusion and misery. The spirit, the law of our mind, takes account of the universal moral order, the will of God, and is indeed the voice of that order expressing itself in us. Paul talks of a man sowing to *his* flesh,[2] because each of us has of his own this individual body, this *congeries* of flesh and bones, blood and nerves, different from that of every one else, and with desires and impulses driving each of us his own separate way ;

[1] *Col.,* iii, 5.   [2] *Gal.,* vi, 8.

and he says that a man who sows to this, sows to a thousand tyrants, and can reap no good harvest. But he talks of sowing to *the* spirit; because there is one central moral tendency which for us and for all men is the law of our being, and through reason and righteousness we move in this universal order and with it. In this conformity, to *the will of God*, as we religiously name the moral order, is our peace and happiness.

But how to find the energy and power to bring all those self-seeking tendencies of the flesh, those multitudinous, swarming, eager, and incessant impulses, into obedience to the central tendency? Mere commanding and forbidding is of no avail, and only irritates opposition in the desires it tries to control. It even enlarges their power, because it makes us feel our impotence; and the confusion caused by their ungoverned working is increased by our being filled with a deepened sense of disharmony, remorse, and dismay. 'I was alive without the law once,'[1] says Paul; the natural play of all the forces and desires in me went on smoothly enough so long as I did not attempt to introduce order and regulation among them. But the condition of immoral tranquillity could not in man be permanent. That natural law of reason and conscience which all men have, was sufficient by itself to produce a consciousness of rebellion and disquietude. Matters became only worse by the exhibition of the Mosaic law, the offspring of a moral sense more poignant and stricter, however little it might show of subtle insight and delicacy, than the moral sense of the mass of mankind. The very stringency of the Mosaic code increased the feeling of dismay and helplessness; it set forth the law of righteousness more authoritatively and minutely, yet did not supply any sufficient power to keep it. Neither the law of nature, therefore, nor the law of Moses, availed

[1] *Rom.*, vii, 9.

to blind men to righteousness. So we come to the word which is in some sense the governing word of the Epistle to the Romans,—the word *all*. As the word *righteousness* is the governing word of St. Paul's entire mind and life, so the word *all* may stand for the governing word of this his chief epistle. The Gentile with the law of nature, the Jew with the law of Moses, alike fail to achieve righteousness. '*All* have sinned, and come short of the glory of God.'[1] All do what they would not, and do not what they would; all feel themselves enslaved, impotent, guilty, miserable. 'O wretched man that I am, who shall deliver me from the body of this death?'[2]

Hitherto, we have followed Paul in the sphere of morals; we have now come with him to the point where he enters the sphere of religion. Religion is that which binds and holds us to the practice of righteousness. We have accompanied Paul, and found him always treading solid ground, till he is brought to straits where a binding and holding power of this kind is necessary. Here is the critical point for the scientific worth of his doctrine. 'Now at last,' cries Puritanism, 'the great apostle is about to become even as one of us; there is no issue for him now, but the issue we have always declared he finds. He has recourse to our theurgy of election, justification, substitution, and imputed righteousness.' We will proceed to show that Paul has recourse to nothing of the kind.

---

[1] *Rom.*, iii, 23. There is a reminiscence of Jeremiah, ix, 25, 26.
[2] *Rom.*, vii, 24.

II.

WE have seen how Puritanism seems to come by its religion in the first instance theologically and from authority; Paul by his, on the other hand, psychologically and from experience. Even the points, therefore, in which they both meet they have not reached in the same order or by the same road. The miserable sense of sin from unrighteousness, the joyful witness of a good conscience from righteousness, these are points in which Puritanism and St. Paul meet. They are facts of human nature and can be verified. But whereas Puritanism, so far as science is concerned, ends with these facts, and rests the whole weight of its antecedent theurgy upon the witness to it they offer, Paul begins with these facts, and has not yet, so far as we have followed him, called upon them to prove anything but themselves. The scientific difference, as we have already remarked, which this establishes between Paul and Puritanism is immense, and is all in Paul's favour. Sin and righteousness, together with their eternal accompaniments of fear and hope, misery and happiness, can prove themselves; but they can by no means prove, also, Puritanism's history of original sin, election and justification.

Puritanism is fond of maintaining, indeed, that Paul's doctrines derive their sanction, not from any agreement with science and experience, but from his miraculous conversion, and that this conversion it was which in his own judgment gave to them their authority. But whatever sanction the miracle of his conversion may in his own eyes have lent to the doctrines afterwards propounded by Paul, it is clear that, for science, his conversion adds to his doctrines no force at all which they do not already possess in themselves. Paul's conversion is for science an event of precisely the same nature as the conversions of which the history of Methodism relates so many; events described, for the most part, just as the event of Paul's conversion is described, with perfect good faith, and which we may perfectly admit to have happened just in the manner related, without on that account attributing to those who underwent them any source of certitude for a scheme of doctrine which this doctrine does not on other and better grounds possess.

Surely this proposition has only to be clearly stated in order to be self-evident. The conversion of Paul is in itself an incident of precisely the same order as the conversion of Sampson Staniforth, a Methodist soldier in the campaign of Fontenoy. Staniforth himself relates his conversion as follows, in words which bear plainly marked on them the very stamp of good faith :—

'From twelve at night till two it was my turn to stand sentinel at a dangerous post. I had a fellow-sentinel, but I desired him to go away, which he willingly did. As soon as I was alone, I knelt down and determined not to rise, but to continue crying and wrestling with God till he had mercy on me. How long I was in that agony I cannot tell ; but as I looked up to heaven I saw the clouds open exceeding bright, and I saw Jesus hanging on the cross. At the same moment these words were applied to my heart : "Thy sins are forgiven thee." All guilt was gone, and my soul was filled with unutterable peace : the fear of death and hell was vanished away. I was filled with wonder and astonishment. I closed my eyes, but the impression was still the same ; and for about ten weeks, while I was awake, let me be where I would, the same appearance was still before my eyes, and the same impression upon my heart: *Thy sins are forgiven thee.*'

Not the narrative, in the *Acts*, of Paul's journey to Damascus, could more convince us, as we have said, of its own honesty. But this honesty makes nothing, as every one will admit, for the scientific truth of any scheme of doctrine propounded by Sampson Staniforth, which must prove itself and its own scientific value before science can admit it. Precisely the same is it with Paul's doctrine; and we repeat, therefore, that he and his doctrine have herein a great advantage over Puritanism, in that, so far as we have yet followed them, they, unlike Puritanism, rely on facts of experience and assert nothing which science cannot verify.

We have now to see whether Paul, in passing from the undoubted facts of experience, with which he begins, to his religion properly so called, abandons in any essential points of his teaching the advantage with which he started, and ends, as Puritanism commences, with a batch of arbitrary and unscientific assumptions.

We left Paul in collision with a fact of human nature, but in itself a sterile fact, a fact on which it is possible to dwell too long, although Puritanism, thinking this impossible, has remained intensely absorbed in the contemplation of it, and indeed has never properly got beyond it,—the sense of sin. Sin is not a monster to be mused on, but an impotence to be got rid of. All thinking about it, beyond what is indispensable for the firm effort to get rid of it, is waste of energy and waste of time. We then enter that element of morbid and subjective brooding, in which so many have perished. This sense of sin, however, it is also possible to have not strongly enough to beget the firm effort to get rid of it, and the Greeks, with all their great gifts, had this sense not strongly enough; its strength in the Hebrew people is one of this people's mainsprings. 'Mine iniquities have taken hold upon me so that I am not able to look up; they are more than the hairs of mine head; therefore my heart faileth me.'[1] *They are more than the hairs of mine head.* The motions of what Paul calls 'the law in our members' are indeed a hydra-brood; when we are working against one fault, a dozen others crop up without our expecting it; and this it is which drives the man who deals seriously with himself to difficulty, nay to despair. Paul did not need James to tell him that whoever offends on one point is, so far at least as his own conscience and inward satisfaction are concerned, guilty of all;[2] he knew it himself, and the unrest this knowledge gave him was his very starting-point. He knew, too, that nothing outward, no satisfaction of all the requirements men may make of us, no privileges of any sort, can give peace of conscience;—of conscience, 'whose praise is not of men but of God.'[3] He knew, also, that the law of the moral order stretches beyond us and our private conscience, is independent of our sense of having kept it, and stands absolute and what in itself it is; even, therefore, though I may know nothing against myself, yet this is not enough, I may still not be just.[4] Finally, Paul knew that merely to know all this and say it, is of no use, advances us nothing; 'the kingdom of God is not in word but in power.'[5]

We have several times said that the Hebrew race apprehended God,—the universal order by which all things fulfil the law of their being,—chiefly as the moral order in human nature, and that it was their greatness that they apprehended him as this so distinctly and powerfully. But it is also characteristic of them, and perhaps it is what mainly distinguishes their spirit from the spirit of mediæval Christianity,

---

[1] *Ps.* xl, 12.   [2] James, ii, 10.   [3] *Rom.*, ii, 29.
[4] 1 *Cor.*, iv, 4.   [5] *Ibid.*, 20.

that they constantly thought, too, of God as the source of life and breath and all things, and of what they called 'fulness of life' in all things. This way of thinking was common to them with the Greeks; although, whereas the Greeks threw more delicacy and imagination into it, the Hebrews threw more energy and vital warmth. But to the Hebrew, as to the Greek, the gift of life, and health, and the world, was divine, as well as the gift of morals. 'God's *righteousness*,' indeed, 'standeth like the strong mountains, his *judgments* are like the great deep; he is a *righteous* judge, strong and patient, who is provoked every day.'[1] This is the Hebrew's first and deepest conception of God,—as the source of the moral order. But God is also, to the Hebrew, the power by which we have been 'upholden ever since we were born,' and whose 'mercy is over all his works.'[2] He is the power that 'saves both man and beast, gives them drink of his pleasures as out of the river,' and with whom is 'the well of life.'[3] In his speech at Athens, Paul shows how full he, too, was of this feeling; and in the famous passage in the first chapter of the Epistle to the Romans, where he asserts the existence of the natural moral law, the source he assigns to this law is not merely God in conscience, the righteous judge, but God in the world and the workings of the world, the eternal and divine power from which all life and wholesome energy proceed.[4]

This element in which we live and move and have our being, which stretches around and beyond the strictly moral element in us, around and beyond the finite sphere of what is originated, measured, and controlled by our own understanding and will,—this infinite element is very present to Paul's thoughts, and makes a profound impression on them. By this element we are receptive and influenced, not origin-

[1] *Ps.* xxxvi, 6; vii, 11.
[2] *Ps.* lxxi, 6; cxlv, 9.
[3] *Ps.* xxxvi, 6, 8, 9.
[4] *Rom.*, i, 19-21.

ative and influencing; now, we all of us receive far more than we originate. Our pleasure from a spring day we do not make; our pleasure, even, from an approving conscience we do not make. And yet we feel that both the one pleasure and the other can, and often do, work with us in a wonderful way for our good. So we get the thought of an impulsion outside ourselves which is at once awful and beneficent. 'No man,' as the Hebrew psalm says, 'hath quickened his own soul.'[1] 'I know,' says Jeremiah, 'that the way of man is not in himself; it is not in man that walketh to direct his steps.'[2] Most true and natural in this feeling; and the greater men are, the more natural is this feeling to them. Great men like Sylla and Napoleon have loved to attribute their success to their fortune, their star; religious great men have loved to say that their sufficiency was of God.[3] Through every great spirit runs a train of feeling of this sort; and the power and depth which there undoubtedly is in Calvinism, comes from Calvinism's being overwhelmed by it. Paul is not, like Calvinism, overwhelmed by it; but it is always before his mind and strongly agitates his thoughts. The voluntary, rational, and human world, of righteousness, moral choice, effort, filled the first place in his spirit. But the necessary, mystical, and divine world, of influence, sympathy, emotion, filled the second; and he could pass naturally from the one world to the other. The presence in Paul of this twofold feeling acted irresistibly upon his doctrine. What he calls 'the power that worketh in us,'[4] and that produces results transcending all our expectations and calculations, he instinctively sought to combine with our personal agencies of reason and conscience.

Of such a mysterious power and its operation some clear notion may be got by anybody who has ever had any over-

[1] *Ps.* xxii, 29.   [2] Jer., x, 23.
[3] II *Cor.*, iii. 5.   [4] *Eph.*, iii, 20.

powering attachment. Every one knows how being in love changes for the time a man's spiritual atmosphere, and makes animation and buoyancy where before there was flatness and dulness. One may even say that this is the reason why being in love is so popular with the whole human race,—because it relieves in so irresistible and delightful a manner the tedium or depression of common-place human life. And not only does it change the atmosphere of our spirits, making air, light, and movement where before was stagnation and gloom, but it also sensibly and powerfully increases our faculties of action. It is matter of the commonest remark how a timid man who is in love will show courage, or an indolent man will show diligence. Nay, a timid man who would be only the more paralysed in a moment of danger by being told that it is his bounden duty as a man to show firmness, and that he must be ruined and disgraced for ever if he does not, will show firmness quite easily from being in love. An indolent man who shrinks back from vigorous effort only the more because he is told and knows that it is a man's business to show energy, and that it is shameful in him if he does not, will show energy quite easily from being in love. This, I say, we learn from the analogy of the most everyday experience;—that a powerful attachment will give a man spirits and confidence which he could by no means call up or command of himself; and that in this mood he can do wonders which would not be possible to him without it.

We have seen how Paul felt himself to be for the sake of righteousness *apprehended*, to use his own expression, by Christ. 'I seek,' he says, 'to apprehend that for which also I am apprehended by Christ.'[1] This for which he is thus apprehended is,—still to use his own words,—*the righteousness of God*; a sense of conformity with the divine moral

[1] *Philipp.*, iii, 12.

order, the will of God, a sense of harmony with this order, of acceptance with God.

In some points Paul had always served this order with a clear conscience. He did not steal, he did not commit adultery. But he was at the same time, he says himself, 'a blasphemer and a persecutor and an insulter,'[1] and the contemplation of Jesus Christ made him see this, impressed it forcibly upon his mind. Here was his greatness, and the worth of his way of appropriating Christ. We have seen how Calvinism, too,—Calvinism which has built itself upon St. Paul,—is a blasphemer, when it speaks of good works done by those who do not hold the Calvinist doctrine. There would need no great sensitiveness of conscience, one would think, to show that Calvinism has often been, also, a persecutor and an insulter. Calvinism, as well as Paul, professes to study Jesus Christ. But the difference between Paul's study of Christ and Calvinism's is this : that Paul by studying Christ got to know himself clearly, and to transform his narrow conception of righteousness ; while Calvinism studies both Christ and Paul after him to no such good purpose.

The particular impression mentioned is, however, but the veriest fragment of the total impression produced on Paul by the contemplation of Christ. The sum and substance of that total impression may best be conveyed by two words :—*without sin.*

We must here revert to what we have already said of the importance, for sound criticism of a man's ideas, of the order in which his ideas come. For us, who approach Christianity through a scholastic theology, it is Christ's divinity which establishes his being without sin. For Paul, who approached Christianity through his personal experience, it was Jesus Christ's being without sin which estab-

---

[1] 1 *Tim.*, i. 13.

lishes his divinity. The large and complete conception of righteousness to which Paul himself had slowly and late, and only by Jesus Christ's help, awakened, in Jesus he seemed to see existing absolutely and naturally. The devotion to this conception which made it meat and drink to carry it into effect, a devotion of which he himself was strongly and deeply conscious, he saw in Jesus still stronger, by far, and deeper than in himself. But for attaining the righteousness of God, for reaching an absolute conformity with the moral order and with God's will, he saw no such impotence existing in Jesus Christ's case as in his own. For Jesus, the uncertain conflict between the law in our members and the law of the spirit did not appear to exist. Those eternal vicissitudes of victory and defeat, which drove Paul to despair, in Jesus were absent. Smoothly and inevitably he followed the real and eternal order, in preference to the momentary and apparent order. Obstacles outside him there were plenty, but obstacles within him there were none. He was led by the spirit of God; he was dead to sin, he lived to God; and in this life to God he persevered even to the cruel bodily death of the cross. As many as are led by the spirit of God, says Paul, are the sons of God.[1] If this is so with even us, who live to God so feebly and who render such an imperfect obedience, how much more is he who lives to God entirely and who renders an unalterable obedience, the unique and only Son of God?

This is undoubtedly the main line of movement which Paul's ideas respecting Jesus Christ follow. He had been trained, however, in the scholastic theology of Judaism, just as we are trained in the scholastic theology of Christianity; would that we were as little embarrassed with our training as he was with his! The Jewish theological doctrine

[1] *Rom.*, viii, 14.

respecting the eternal word or wisdom of God, which was with God from the beginning before the oldest of his works, and through which the world was created, this doctrine, which appears in the Book of Proverbs and again in the Book of Wisdom,[1] Paul applied to Jesus Christ, and in the Epistle to the Colossians there is a remarkable passage[2] with clear signs of his thus applying it. But then this metaphysical and theological basis to the historic being of Jesus is something added by Paul from outside to his own essential ideas concerning him, something which fitted them and was naturally taken on to them; it is secondary, it is not an original part of his system, much less the ground of it. It fills a very different place in his system from the place which it fills in the system of the author of the Fourth Gospel, who takes his starting-point from it. Paul's starting-point, it cannot be too often repeated, is the idea of righteousness; and his concern with Jesus is as the clue to righteousness, not as the clue to transcendental ontology. Speculations in this region had no overpowering attraction for Paul, notwithstanding the traces of an acquaintance with them which we find in his writings, and notwithstanding the great activity of his intellect. This activity threw itself with an unerring instinct into a sphere where, with whatever travail and through whatever impediments to clear expression, directly practical religious results might yet be won, and not into any sphere of abstract speculation.

Much more visible and important than his identification of Jesus with the divine hypostasis known as the Logos, is Paul's identification of him with the Messiah. Ever present is his recognition of him as the Messiah to whom all the law and prophets pointed, of whom the heart of the Jewish race was full, and on whom the Jewish instructors of Paul's youth had dwelt abundantly. The Jewish lan-

[1] *Prov.*, viii, 22-31; and *Wisd.*, vii, 25-27.   [2] *Col.*, i, 15-17.

guage and ideas respecting the end of the world and the Messiah's kingdom, his day, his presence, his appearing, his glory, Paul applied to Jesus, and constantly used. Of the force and reality which these ideas and expressions had for him there can be no question; as to his use of them, only two remarks are needed. One is, that in him these Jewish ideas,—as any one will feel who calls to mind a genuine display of them like that in the Apocalypse,—are spiritualised; and as he advances in his course they are spiritualised increasingly. The other remark is, that important as these ideas are in Paul, of them, too, the importance is only secondary, compared with that of the great central matter of his thoughts: *the righteousness of God, the non-fulfilment of it by man, the fulfilment of it by Christ.*

Once more we are led to a result favourable to the scientific value of Paul's teaching. That Jesus Christ was the divine Logos, the second person of the Trinity, science can neither deny nor affirm. That he was the Jewish Messiah, who will some day appear in the sky with the sound of trumpets, to put an end to the actual kingdoms of the world and to establish his own kingdom, science can neither deny nor affirm. The very terms of which these propositions are composed are such as science is unable to handle. But that the Jesus of the Bible follows the universal moral order and the will of God, without being let and hindered as we are by the motions of private passion and by self-will, this is evident to whoever can read the Bible with open eyes. It is just what any criticism of the Gospel-history, which sees that history as it really is, tells us; it is the scientific result of that history. And this is the result which pre-eminently occupies Paul. Of Christ's life and death, the all-importance for us according to Paul is that by means of them, 'denying ungodliness and worldly lusts, we should live soberly, righteously, and godly;' should be enabled to 'bear fruit to God' in 'love, joy, peace, patience, kindness, goodness, faith, mildness, self-control.'[1] Of Christ's life and death the scope was 'to redeem us from all iniquity, and make us purely zealous for good works.'[2] Paul says that we are to live thus in the actual world which now is, 'with the expectation of the appearing of the glory of God and Christ.'[3] By nature and habit, and with his full belief that the end of the world was nigh at hand, Paul used these words to mean a Messianic coming and kingdom. Later Christianity has transferred them, as it has transferred so much else of Paul's, to a life beyond the grave, but it has by no means spiritualised them. Paul, as his spiritual growth advanced, spiritualised them more and more; he came to think, in using them, more and more of a gradual inward transformation of the world by a conformity like Christ's to the will of God, than of a Messianic advent. Yet even then they are always second with him, and not first; the essence of saving grace is always to make us righteous, to bring us into conformity with the divine law, to enable us to 'bear fruit to God.'

'Jesus Christ gave himself for us that he might redeem us from iniquity.' First of all, he rendered an unbroken obedience to the law of the spirit; he served the spirit of God; he came, not to do his own will, but the will of God. Now, the law of the spirit makes men one; it is only by the law in our members that we are many. Secondly, therefore, Jesus Christ had an unfailing sense of what we have called, using an expressive modern term, the *solidarity* of men: that it was not God's will that one of his human creatures should perish. Thirdly, Jesus Christ persevered in this uninterrupted obedience to the law of the spirit, in this unfailing sense of human solidarity, even to the death; though everything

---

[1] *Tit.*, ii, 12; *Rom.*, vii, 4; *Gal.*, v, 22, 23.
[2] *Tit.*, ii, 14.   [3] *Ibid.*, 13.

befel him which might break the one or tire out the other. Lastly, he had in himself, in all he said and did, that ineffable force of attraction which doubled the virtue of everything said or done by him.

If ever there was a case in which the wonder-working power of attachment, in a man for whom the moral sympathies and the desire of righteousness were all-powerful, might employ itself and work its wonders, it was here. Paul felt this power penetrate him; and he felt, also, how by perfectly identifying himself through it with Jesus, by appropriating Jesus, and in no other way, could he ever get the confidence and the force to do as Jesus did. He thus found a point in which the mighty world outside man, and the weak world inside him, seemed to combine for his salvation. The struggling stream of duty, which had not volume enough to bear him to his goal, was suddenly reinforced by the immense tidal wave of sympathy and emotion.

To this new and potent influence Paul gave the name of *faith*. More fully he calls it: 'Faith that worketh *through love*.'[1] The essential meaning of the word *faith* is 'power of holding on to the unseen,' 'fidelity.' Other attachments demand fidelity in absence to an object which at some time or other, nevertheless, has been seen; this attachment demands fidelity to an object which both is absent and has never been seen by us. It is therefore rightly called not constancy, but faith; a power, pre-eminently, of *holding fast to an unseen power of goodness*. Identifying ourselves with Jesus Christ through this attachment we become as he was. We appropriate him, we live with his thoughts and feelings, and we participate, therefore, in his freedom from the ruinous law in our members, in his obedience to the saving law of the spirit, in his conformity to the eternal order, in the joy and peace of his life to God. 'The law of the spirit of life

[1] *Gal.*, v, 6.

in Christ Jesus,' says Paul, 'frees me from the law of sin and death.'[1] This is what is done for us by *faith*.

It is evident that Paul adds to the general sense of the word faith,—*a holding fast to an unseen power of goodness,*—a particular sense of his own,—*through identification with Christ*. It will at once appear that this faith of Paul's is in truth a specific form of holding fast to an unseen power of goodness; and that while it can properly be said of Abraham, for instance, that he was justified by faith, if we take faith in its plain sense of holding fast to an unseen power of goodness, yet it cannot without difficulty and recourse to a strained figure be said of him, if we take faith in Paul's specific sense of identification with Christ through the emotion of attachment to him. Paul however, undoubtedly, having conveyed his new specific sense into the word faith, still uses the word both in the specific sense of identification with Christ and also in all cases where, without this specific sense, it was before applicable and usual; and in this way he often creates ambiguity. Why, it may be asked, does Paul, instead of employing another term to denote his special meaning, still thus employ the general term faith? We are inclined to think it was from that desire to get for his words and thoughts not only the real but also the apparent sanction and consecration of the Hebrew Scriptures, which we have called his tendency to Judaise. It was written of the founder of Israel, Abraham, that he *believed* God and it was counted to him for righteousness. The prophet Habakkuk had the famous text: 'The just shall live by *faith*.'[2] Jesus, too, had used and sanctioned the use of the word *faith* to signify cleaving to the unseen God's power of goodness as shown in Christ.[3] Peter and John and the other apostles habitually used the word in the same sense, with the modification

---

[1] *Rom.*, viii, 2.   [2] *Gen.*, xv, 6; Habakkuk, ii, 4.
[3] Mark, xi, 22.

introduced by Christ's departure. This was enough to make Paul retain for that vital operation, which was the heart of his whole religious system, the name of faith, though he had considerably developed and enlarged the name's usual meaning. Fraught with this new and developed sense, the term does not always quite well suit the cases to which it was in its old sense, with perfect propriety, applied; this, however, Paul did not regard. The term applied with undeniable truth, though not with perfect adequacy, to the great spiritual operation whereto he affixed it; and it was at the same time the name given to the crowning grace of the great father of the Jewish nation, Abraham; it was the prophet Habakkuk's talismanic and consecrated term, *faith.*

In this word *faith,* as used by St. Paul,[1] we reach a point round which the ceaseless stream of religious exposition and discussion has for ages circled. Even for those who misconceive Paul's line of ideas most completely, faith is so evidently the central point in his system that their thoughts cannot but centre upon it. Puritanism, as is well known, has talked of little else but faith. And the word is of such a nature, that the true clue once lost which Paul has given us to its meaning, every man may put into it almost anything he likes, all the fancies of his superstition or of his fanaticism. To say, therefore, that to have faith in Christ means to be attached to Christ, to embrace Christ, to appropriate Christ, to be identified with Christ, is not enough; the question is, to be attached to him *how,* to embrace him *how?*

A favourite expression of popular theology conveys perfectly the popular definition of faith: *to rest in the finished*

---

[1] With secondary uses of the word, such as its use with the article, '*the* faith,' in expressions like 'the words of the faith,' to signify the body of tenets and principles received by believers from the apostle, we need not here concern ourselves. They present no difficulty.

work of the Saviour. In the scientific language of Protestant theology, to embrace Christ, to have saving faith, is 'to give our consent heartily to the covenant of grace, and so to receive the benefit of justification, whereby God pardons all our sins and accepts us as righteous for the righteousness of Christ imputed to us.' This is mere theurgy, in which, so far as we have yet gone, we have not found Paul dealing. Wesley, with his genius for godliness, struggled all his life for some deeper and more edifying account of that faith, which he felt working wonders in his own soul, than that it was a hearty consent to the covenant of grace and an acceptance of the benefit of Christ's imputed righteousness. Yet this amiable and gracious spirit, but intellectually slight and shallow compared to Paul, beat his wings in vain. Paul, nevertheless, had solved the problem for him, if only he could have had eyes to see Paul's solution.

'He that believes in Christ,' says Wesley, 'discerns spiritual things: he is enabled to taste, see, hear, and feel God.' There is nothing practical and solid here. A company of Cornish revivalists will have no difficulty in tasting, seeing, hearing, and feeling God, twenty times over, to-night, and yet may be none the better for it to-morrow morning. When Paul said, *In Jesus Christ neither circumcision availeth anything nor uncircumcision, but faith that worketh through love; Have faith in Christ!* these words did not mean for him: 'Give your hearty belief and consent to the covenant of grace; Receive the offered benefit of justification through Christ's imputed righteousness.' They did not mean: 'Try and discern spiritual things, try and taste, see, hear, and feel God.' They did not mean: 'Rest in the finished work of Christ the Saviour.' No, they meant: *Die with him!*

The object of this treatise is not religious edification, but the true criticism of a great and misunderstood author. Yet it is impossible to be in presence of this Pauline conception of faith without remarking on the incomparable power of edification which it contains. It is indeed a crowning evidence of that piercing practical religious sense which we have attributed to Paul. It is at once mystical and rational; and it enlists in its service the best forces of both worlds,— the world of reason and morals, and the world of sympathy and emotion. The world of reason and duty has an excellent clue to action, but wants motive-power: the world of sympathy and influence has an irresistible force of motive-power, but wants a clue for directing its exertion. The danger of the one world is weariness in well-doing; the danger of the other is sterile raptures and immoral fanaticism. Paul takes from both worlds what can help him, and leaves what cannot. The elemental power of sympathy and emotion in us, a power which extends beyond the limits of our own will and conscious activity, which we cannot measure and control, and which in each of us differs immensely in force, volume, and mode of manifestation, he calls into full play, and sets it to work with all its strength and in all its variety. But one unalterable object is assigned by him to this power: *to die with Christ to the law of the flesh, to live with Christ to the law of the mind.*

This is the doctrine of the *necrosis*,[1]—Paul's central doctrine, and the doctrine which makes his profoundness and originality. His repeated and minute lists of practices and feelings to be followed or suppressed, now take a heightened significance. They were the matter by which his faith tried itself and knew itself. Those multitudinous motions of appetite and self-will which reason and conscience disapproved, reason and conscience could yet not govern, and had to yield to them. This, as we have seen, is what drove Paul almost to despair. Well, then, how did Paul's faith,

[1] II *Cor.*, iv, 10.

working through love, help him here? It enabled him to reinforce duty by affection. In the central need of his nature, the desire to govern these motions of unrighteousness, it enabled him to say: *Die to them! Christ did.* If any man be in Christ, said Paul—that is, if any man identifies himself with Christ by attachment so that he appropriates him, enters into his feelings and lives with his life,—he is a new creature;[1] he can do, and does, what Christ did. First, he suffers with him. Christ throughout his life and in his death presented his body a living sacrifice to God; every self-willed impulse blindly trying to assert itself without respect of the universal order, he died to. You, says Paul to his disciple, are to do the same. Never mind how various and multitudinous the impulses are; impulses to intemperance, concupiscence, covetousness, pride, sloth, envy, malignity, anger, clamour, bitterness, harshness, unmercifulness. Die to them all, and to each as it comes! Christ did. If you cannot, your attachment, your faith, must be one that goes but a very little way. In an ordinary human attachment, you can often suppress quite easily, because by sympathy you enter into another's feelings, this or that impulse of selfishness which happens to conflict with them, and which hitherto you have obeyed. *All* impulses of selfishness conflict with Christ's feelings, he showed it by dying to them all; if you are one with him by faith and sympathy, you can die to them also. Then, secondly, if you thus die with him, you become transformed by the renewing of your mind, and rise with him. The law of the spirit of life which is in Christ becomes the law of your life also, and frees you from the law of sin and death. You rise with him to that harmonious conformity with the real and eternal order, that sense of pleasing God who trieth the hearts, which is life and peace, and which grows more and more till it becomes glory. If you

[1] II *Cor.*, v, 17.

suffer with him, therefore, you shall also be glorified with him.

The real worth of this mystical conception depends on the fitness of the character and history of Jesus Christ for inspiring such attachment and devotion as that which Paul's notion of faith implies. If the character and history are eminently such as to inspire it, then Paul has no doubt found a mighty aid towards the attainment of that righteousness of which Jesus Christ's life afforded the admirable pattern. A great solicitude is always shown by popular Christianity to establish a radical difference between Jesus and a teacher like Socrates. Ordinary theologians establish this difference by transcendental distinctions into which science cannot follow them. But what makes for scientific criticism the radical difference between Jesus and Socrates, is that such a conception as Paul's would, if applied to Socrates, be out of place and ineffective. Socrates inspired boundless friendship and esteem; but the inspiration of reason and conscience is the one inspiration which comes from him, and which impels us to live righteously as he did. A penetrating enthusiasm of love, sympathy, pity, adoration, reinforcing the inspiration of reason and duty, does not belong to Socrates. With Jesus it is different. On this point it is needless to argue; history has proved. In the midst of errors the most prosaic, the most immoral, the most unscriptural, concerning God, Christ, and righteousness, the immense emotion of love and sympathy inspired by the person and character of Jesus has had to work almost by itself alone for righteousness; and it has worked wonders. The surpassing religious grandeur of Paul's conception of faith is that it seizes a real salutary emotional force of incalculable magnitude, and reinforces moral effort with it.

Paul's mystical conception is not complete without its relation of us to our fellow men, as well as its relation of us to Jesus Christ. Whoever identifies himself with Christ, identifies himself with Christ's idea of the solidarity of men. The whole race is conceived as one body, having to die and rise with Christ, and forming by the joint action of its regenerate members the mystical body of Christ. Hence the truth of that which Bishop Wilson says : 'It is not so much our neighbour's interest as our own that we love him.' Jesus Christ's life, with which we by faith identify ourselves, is not complete, his aspiration after the eternal order is not satisfied, so long as only Jesus himself follows this order, or only this or that individual amongst us men follows it. The same law of emotion and sympathy, therefore, which prevails in our inward self-discipline, is to prevail in our dealings with others. The motions of sin in ourselves we succeed in mortifying, not by saying to ourselves that they are forbidden, but by sympathy with Christ in his mortification of them. In like manner, our duties towards our neighbour we perform, not in deference to external commands and prohibitions, but through identifying ourselves with him by sympathy with Christ who identified himself with him. Therefore, we owe no man anything but to love one another ; and he who loves his neighbour fulfils the law towards him, because he seeks to do him good and forbears to do him harm just as if he was himself.

Mr. Lecky cannot see that the command to speak the truth to one's neighbour is a command which has a natural sanction. But according to these Pauline ideas it has a clear natural sanction. For, if my neighbour is merely an extension of myself, deceiving my neighbour is the same as deceiving myself ; and than self-deceit there is nothing by nature more baneful. And on this ground Paul puts the injunction. He says : 'Speak every man truth to his neighbour, *for* we are members one of another.'[1] This direction

[1] *Eph.*, iv, 25.

ST. PAUL AND PROTESTANTISM. 55

to identify ourselves in Jesus Christ with our neighbours is hard and startling, no doubt, like the direction to identify ourselves with Jesus and die with him. But it is also, like that direction, inspiring; and not, like a set of mere mechanical commands and prohibitions, lifeless and unaiding. It shows a profound practical religious sense, and rests upon facts of human nature which experience can follow and appreciate.

The three essential terms of Pauline theology are not, therefore, as popular theology makes them : *calling, justification, sanctification.* They are rather these : *dying with Christ, resurrection from the dead, growing into Christ.*[1] The order in which these terms are placed indicates, what we have already pointed out elsewhere, the true Pauline sense of the expression, *resurrection from the dead.* In Paul's ideas the expression has no essential connexion with physical death. It is true, popular theology connects it with this almost exclusively, and regards any other use of it as purely figurative and secondary. For popular theology, Christ's resurrection is his bodily resurrection in Jerusalem after his physical death on the cross ; the believer's resurrection is his bodily resurrection in a future world, the golden city of our hymns and of the Apocalypse. For this theology, the force of Christ's resurrection is that it is a miracle which guarantees the promised future miracle of our own resurrection. It is a common remark with Biblical critics, even with able and candid Biblical critics, that Christ's resurrection, in this sense of a physical miracle, is the central object of Paul's thoughts and the foundation of all his theology. Nay, the preoccupation with this idea has altered the very text of our documents ; so that whereas Paul wrote, 'Christ died and lived,' we read, 'Christ died

[1] ἀποθανεῖν σὺν Χριστῷ, *Col.*, ii, 20 ; ἐξανάστασις ἐκ νεκρῶν, *Philipp.*, iii, 11 ; αὔξησις εἰς Χριστόν, *Eph.*, iv, 15.

and rose again and revived.'[1] But whoever has carefully followed Paul's line of thought as we have endeavoured to trace it, will see that in his mature theology, as the Epistle to the Romans exhibits it, it cannot be this physical and miraculous aspect of the resurrection which holds the first place in his mind; for under this aspect the resurrection does not fit in with the ideas which he is developing.

Not for a moment do we deny that in Paul's earlier theology, and notably in the Epistles to the Thessalonians and Corinthians, the physical and miraculous aspect of the resurrection, both Christ's and the believer's, is primary and predominant. Not for a moment do we deny that to the very end of his life, after the Epistle to the Romans, after the Epistle to the Philippians, if he had been asked whether he held the doctrine of the resurrection in the physical and miraculous sense, as well as in his own spiritual and mystical sense, he would have replied with entire conviction that he did. Very likely it would have been impossible to him to imagine his theology without it. But:—

> Below the surface-stream, shallow and light,
> Of what we *say* we feel—below the stream,
> As light, of what we *think* we feel—there flows
> With noiseless current strong, obscure and deep,
> The central stream of what we feel indeed;

and by this alone are we truly characterised. Paul's originality lies in the effort to find a moral side and significance for all the processes, however mystical, of the religious life, with a view of strengthening, in this way, their hold upon us and their command of all our nature. Sooner or later he was sure to be drawn to treat the process of resurrection with this endeavour. He did so treat it; and what is original and essential in him is his doing so.

Paul's conception of life and death inevitably came to

[1] *Rom.*, xiv, 9.

govern his conception of resurrection. What indeed, as we have seen, is for Paul life, and what is death? Not the ordinary physical life and death. Death, for him, is living after the flesh, obedience to sin; life is mortifying by the spirit the deeds of the flesh, obedience to righteousness. Resurrection, in its essential sense, is therefore for Paul the rising, within the sphere of our visible earthly existence, from death in this sense to life in this sense. It is indubitable that, so far as the human believer's resurrection is concerned, this is so. Else, how could Paul say to the Colossians (to take only one out of many clear texts showing the same thing): '*If ye then be risen with Christ*, seek the things that are above.'[1] But when Paul repeats again and again, in the Epistle to the Romans, that the matter of our faith is 'that God raised Jesus from the dead,' the essential meaning of this resurrection, also, is just the same. Real life, for Paul, begins with the mystical death which frees us from the dominion of the external *shalls* and *shall nots* of the law.[2] From the moment, therefore, that Jesus Christ was content to do God's will, he died. Paul's point is, that Jesus Christ in his earthly existence obeyed the law of the spirit and bore fruit to God; and that the believer should, in his earthly existence, do the same. That Christ 'died to sin,' that he 'pleased not himself,' and that, consequently, through all his life here, he was risen and living to God, is what occupies Paul. Christ's physical resurrection after he was crucified is neither in point of time nor in point of character the resurrection on which Paul, following his essential line of thought, wanted to fix the believer's mind. The resurrection Paul was striving after for himself and others was a resurrection *now*, and a resurrection to *righteousness*.[3]

[1] *Col.*, iii, 1.   [2] See *Rom.*, vii, 1-6.
[3] It has been said that this was the error of Hymenæus and Philetas (II *Tim.*, ii, 17). It might be rejoined, with much plausibility, that

But Jesus Christ's obeying God and not pleasing himself culminated in his death on the cross. All through his career, indeed, Jesus Christ pleased not himself and died to sin. But so smoothly and so inevitably, as we have before said, did he always appear to follow that law of the moral order, which to us it costs such effort to obey, that only in the very wrench and pressure of his violent death did any pain of dying, any conflict between the law of the flesh and the law of the spirit, in Christ become visible. But the Christian needs to find in Christ's dying to sin a fellowship of suffering and a conformity of death. Well, then, the point of Christ's trial and crucifixion is the only point in his career where the Christian can palpably touch what he seeks. In all dying there is struggle and weakness; in our dying to sin there is great struggle and weakness. But only in his crucifixion can we see, in Jesus Christ, a place for struggle and weakness.[1] That self-sacrificing obedience of Jesus Christ's whole life, which was summed up in this great, final act of his crucifixion, and which is palpable as sacrifice, obedience, dolorous effort, only there, is therefore constantly regarded by Paul under the figure of this final act, as is also the believer's conformity to Christ's obedience. The believer is crucified with Christ when he mortifies by the spirit the deeds of unrighteousness; Christ was crucified

their error was the error of popular theology, the fixing the attention on the past miracle of Christ's physical resurrection, and losing sight of the continuing miracle of the Christian's spiritual resurrection. Probably, however, Hymenæus and Philetas controverted some of Paul's tenets respecting the approaching Messianic advent and the resurrection then to take place (1 *Thess.*, iv, 13-17). If they rejected these tenets, they were right where Paul was wrong. But if they disputed and separated on account of them, they were *heretics*; that is, they had their hearts and minds full of a speculative contention, instead of their proper chief-concern,—*putting on the new man*, and the imitation of Christ.

[1] ἐσταυρώθη ἐξ ἀσθενείας, II *Cor.*, xiii, 4.

when he pleased not himself, and came to do not his own will but God's.

It is the same with life as with death; it turns on no physical event, but on that central concern of Paul's thoughts, righteousness. If we have the spirit of Christ, we live, as he did, by the spirit, 'serve the spirit of God,'[1] and follow the eternal order. The spirit of God, the spirit of Christ, is the same,—the one eternal moral order. If we are led by the spirit of God we are the sons of God, and share with Christ the heritage of the sons of God,—eternal life, peace, felicity, glory. The spirit, therefore, is life *because of righteousness.* And when, through identifying ourselves with Christ, we reach Christ's righteousness, then eternal life begins for us; —a continuous and ascending life, for the eternal order never dies, and the more we transform ourselves into servants of righteousness and organs of the eternal order, the more we are and desire to be this eternal order and nothing else. Even in this life we are 'seated in heavenly places,'[2] as Christ is; so entirely, for Paul, is righteousness the true life and the true heaven. But the transformation cannot be completed here; the physical death is regarded by Paul as a stage at which it ceases to be impeded. However, at this stage we quit, as he himself says, the ground of experience and enter upon the ground of hope. But, by a sublime analogy, he fetches from the travail of the whole universe proof of the necessity and beneficence of the law of transformation. Jesus Christ entered into his glory when he had made his physical death itself a crowning witness to his obedience to righteousness; we, in like manner, within the limits of this earthly life and before we have yet persevered to the end, must not look for full adoption, for the glorious revelation in us of the sons of God.[3]

[1] According to the true reading in *Philipp.*, iii, 3.
[2] *Eph.*, ii, 6. [3] *Rom.*, viii, 18-25.

That Paul, as we have said, accepted the physical miracle of Christ's resurrection and ascension as a part of the signs and wonders which accompanied Christianity, there can be no doubt. Just in the same manner he accepted the eschatology, as it is called, of his nation,—their doctrine of the final things and of the summons by a trumpet in the sky to judgment; he accepted Satan, hierarchies of angels, and an approaching end of the world. What we deny is, that his acceptance of the former gives to his teaching its essential characters, any more than his acceptance of the latter. We should but be continuing, with strict logical development, Paul's essential line of thought, if we said that the true ascension and glorified reign of Christ was the triumph and reign of his spirit, of his real life, far more operative after his death on the cross than before it; and that in this sense, most truly, he and all who persevere to the end as he did are 'sown in weakness but raised in power.' Paul himself, however, did not distinctly continue his thought thus, and neither will we do so for him. How far Paul himself knew that he had gone in his irresistible bent to find, for each of the data of his religion, that side of moral and spiritual significance which, as a mere sign and wonder, it had not and could not have,— what data he himself was conscious of having transferred, through following this bent, from the first rank in importance to the second,—we cannot know with any certainty. That the bent existed, that Paul felt it existed, and that it establishes a wide difference between the earliest epistles and the latest, is beyond question. Already, in the Second Epistle to the Corinthians, he declares that, 'though he had known Christ after the flesh, yet henceforth he knew him so no more;'[1] and in the Epistle to the Romans, shortly

---

[1] II *Cor.* v, 16.

ST. PAUL AND PROTESTANTISM. 61

afterwards, he rejects the notion of dwelling on the miraculous Christ, on the descent into hell and on the ascent into heaven, and fixes the believer's attention solely on the faith of Christ and on the effects produced by an acquaintance with it.[1] In the same Epistle, in like manner, the kingdom of God, of which to the Thessalonians he described the advent in such materialising and popularly Judaic language, has become 'righteousness, and peace, and joy in the holy spirit.'[2]

These ideas, we repeat, may never have excluded others, which absorbed the most part of Paul's contemporaries as they absorb popular religion at this day. To popular religion, the real kingdom of God is the New Jerusalem with its jaspers and emeralds ; righteousness and peace and joy are only the kingdom of God figuratively. The real sitting in heavenly places is the sitting on thrones in a land of pure delight after we are dead ; serving the spirit of God is only sitting in heavenly places figuratively. Science exactly reverses this process. For science, the spiritual notion is the real one, the material notion is figurative. The astonishing greatness of Paul is, that, coming when and where and whence he did, he yet grasped the spiritual notion, if not exclusively and fully, yet firmly and predominantly ; more and more predominantly through all the last years of his life. And what makes him original and himself, is not what he shares with his contemporaries and with modern popular religion, but this which he develops of his own ; and this which he develops of his own is just of a nature to make his religion a theology instead of a theurgy, and at bottom a scientific instead of a non-scientific structure. 'Die and come to life !' says Goethe,—an unsuspected witness, assuredly, to the psychological and scientific profoundness of Paul's

---

[1] *Rom.*, x, 6-10.   [2] *Rom.*, xiv, 17.

conception of life and death :—'Die and come to life ! for, so long as this is not accomplished, thou art but a troubled guest upon an earth of gloom.'[1]

The three cardinal points in Paul's theology are not therefore, we repeat, those commonly assigned by Puritanism, *calling, justification, sanctification*; but they are these : *dying with Christ, resurrection from the dead, growing into Christ*. And we will venture, moreover, to affirm that the more the Epistle to the Romans is read and re-read with a clear mind, the more will the conviction strengthen, that the essential sense in which Paul in his Epistle to the Romans uses the term *resurrection* is that of a rising, in this visible earthly existence, from the death of obedience to blind selfish impulse, to the life of obedience to the eternal moral order;—in Christ's case first, as the pattern for us to follow; in the believer's case afterwards, as following Christ's pattern through identifying himself with him.

We have thus reached Paul's fundamental conception without even a glimpse of the fundamental conceptions of Puritanism, which, nevertheless, professes to have learnt its doctrine from St. Paul and from his Epistle to the Romans. Once, for a moment, the term *faith* brought us in contact with the doctrine of Puritanism, but only to see that the essential sense given to this word by Paul Puritanism had missed entirely. Other parts, then, of the Epistle to the Romans than those by which we have been occupied must have chiefly fixed the attention of Puritanism. And so it has in truth been. Yet the parts of the Epistle to the Romans that have occupied us are undoubtedly the parts which not our own theories and inclinations,—for we have

[1] Stirb und werde !
Denn so lang du das nicht hast,
Bist du nur ein trüber Gast
Auf der dunkeln Erde.

approached the matter without admitting any,—but an impartial criticism of Paul's real line of thought, must elevate as the most important. If a somewhat pedantic form of expression may be forgiven for the sake of clearness, we may say that of the eleven first chapters of the Epistle to the Romans,—the chapters which convey Paul's theology, though not, as we have seen, with any scholastic purpose, or in any formal scientific mode of exposition,—of these eleven chapters, the first, second, and third are, in a scale of importance fixed by a scientific criticism of Paul's line of thought, sub-primary; the fourth and fifth are secondary; the sixth and eighth are primary; the seventh chapter is sub-primary; the ninth, tenth, and eleventh chapters are secondary. Furthermore, to the contents of the separate chapters themselves this scale must be carried on, so far as to mark that of the two great primary chapters, the sixth and the eighth, the eighth is primary down only to the end of the twenty-eighth verse; from thence to the end it is, however eloquent, yet, for the purpose of a scientific criticism of Paul's essential theology, only secondary.

The first chapter is to the Gentiles. Its purport is: You have not righteousness. The second is to the Jews; and its purport is: No more have you, though you think you have. The third chapter announces faith in Christ as the one source of righteousness for all men. The fourth chapter gives to the notion of righteousness through faith the sanction of the Old Testament and of the history of Abraham. The fifth insists on the causes for thankfulness and exultation in the boon of righteousness through faith in Christ; and applies illustratively, with this design, the history of Adam. The sixth chapter comes to the all-important question: 'What *is* that faith in Christ which I, Paul, mean?'—and answers it. The seventh illustrates and explains the answer. But the eighth, down to the end of the twenty-eighth verse, develops and completes the answer. The rest of the eighth chapter expresses the sense of safety and gratitude which the solution is fitted to inspire. The ninth, tenth, and eleventh chapters uphold the second chapter's thesis,—so hard to a Jew, so easy to us,—that righteousness is not by the Jewish law; but dwell with hope and joy on a final result of things which is to be favourable to Israel.

We shall be pardoned this somewhat formal analysis in consideration of the clearness with which it enables us to survey the Puritan scheme of original sin, predestination, and justification. The historical transgression of Adam occupies, it will be observed, in Paul's ideas by no means the primary, fundamental, all-important place which it holds in the ideas of Puritanism. 'This' (the transgression of Adam) 'is our original sin, the bitter root of all our actual transgressions in thought, word, and deed.' Paul did not go to Adam and Genesis to get the essential testimony about sin. He went to experience for it. 'I *see*,' he says, 'a law in my members fighting against the law of my mind, and bringing me into captivity.'[1] This is the essential testimony respecting sin to Paul,—this rise of sin in his own heart and in the heart of all the men who hear him. At quite a later stage in his conception of the religious life, in quite a subordinate capacity, and for the mere purpose of illustration, comes in the allusion to Adam and to what is called original sin. Paul's desire for righteousness has carried him to Christ and to the conception of the righteousness which is of God by faith, and he is expressing his gratitude, delight, wonder, at the boon he has discovered. For the purpose of exalting it he reverts to the well-known story of Adam. It cannot even be said that Paul Judaises in his use here of this story; so entirely does he subor-

[1] *Rom.*, vii, 23.

dinate it to his purpose of illustration, using it just as he might have used it had he believed, which undoubtedly he did not, that he was using merely a symbolical legend, possessing the advantage of being perfectly familiar to himself and his hearers. 'Think,' he says, 'how in Adam's fall one man's one transgression involved all men in punishment; then estimate the blessedness of our boon in Christ, where one man's one righteousness involves a world of transgressors in blessing!'[1] This is not a scientific doctrine of corruption inherited through Adam's fall; it is a rhetorical use of Adam's fall in a passing allusion to it.

We come to predestination. We have seen how strong was Paul's consciousness of that power, *not ourselves*, in which we live and move and have our being. The sense of life, peace, and joy, which comes through identification with Christ, brings with it a deep and grateful consciousness that this sense is none of our own getting and making. No, it is grace, it is the free gift of God, who gives abundantly beyond all that we ask or think, and calls things that are not as though they were. 'It is not of him that willeth or of him that runneth, but of God that showeth mercy.'[2] As self-moved agents, for whom alone exist all the predicaments of merit and demerit, praise and blame, vice and virtue, we are impotent and lost;—we are saved through that in us which is passive and involuntary; we are saved through our affections, it is by an *influence* and emotion that we are saved! Well might Paul cry out, as this mystical but profound and beneficent conception filled his soul: 'All things work together for good to them that love God, to them who are the called according to his purpose.'[3] Well might he say, in the gratitude which cannot find words enough to express its sense of boundless favour, that those who reach peace with God through identifica-

[1] *Rom.*, v, 12-21.   [2] *Rom.*, ix, 16.   [3] *Rom.*, viii, 28.

tion with Jesus Christ are vessels of mercy, marked from endless ages; that they have been foreknown, predestinated, called, justified, glorified.

It may be regretted, for the sake of the clear understanding of his essential doctrine, that Paul did not stop here. It might seem as if the word 'prothesis,' *purpose*, lured him on into speculative mazes, and involved him, at last, in an embarrassment, from which he impatiently tore himself by the harsh and unedifying image of the clay and the potter. But this is not so. These allurements of speculation, which have been fatal to so many of his interpreters, never mastered Paul. He was led into difficulty by the tendency which we have already noticed as making his real imperfection both as a thinker and as a writer,—the tendency to Judaise.

Already, in the fourth chapter, this tendency had led him to seem to rest his doctrine of justification by faith upon the case of Abraham, whereas, in truth, it needs all the good will in the world, and some effort of ingenuity, even to bring the case of Abraham within the operation of this doctrine. That righteousness is life, that all men by themselves fail of righteousness, that only through identification with Jesus Christ can they reach it,—these propositions, for us at any rate, prove themselves much better than they are proved by the thesis that Abraham in old age believed God's promise that his seed should yet be as the stars for multitude, and that this was counted to him for righteousness. The sanction thus apparently given to the idea that faith is a mere belief, or opinion of the mind, has put thousands of Paul's readers on a false track.

But Paul's Judaising did not end here. To establish his doctrine of righteousness by faith, he had to eradicate the notion that his people were specially privileged, and that, having the Mosaic law, they did not need anything farther.

For us, this one verse of the tenth chapter : *There is no difference between Jew and Greek, for it is the same Lord of all, who is rich to all that call upon him,*—and these four words of another verse : *For righteousness, heart-faith necessary !*—effect far more for Paul's object than his three chapters bristling with Old Testament quotations. By quotation, however, he was to proceed, in order to invest his doctrine with the talismanic virtues of a verbal sanction from the law and the prophets. He shows, therefore, that the law and the prophets had said that only a remnant, an *elect remnant*, of Israel should be saved, and that the rest should be blinded. But to say that peace with God through Jesus Christ inspires such an abounding sense of gratitude, and of its not being our own work, that we can only speak of ourselves as *called* and *chosen* to it, is one thing ; in so speaking, we are on the ground of personal experience. To say, on the other hand, that God has blinded and reprobated other men, so that they shall not reach this blessing, is to quit the ground of personal experience, and to begin employing the magnified and non-natural man in the next street. We then require, in order to account for his proceedings, such an analogy as that of the clay and the potter.

This is Calvinism, and St. Paul undoubtedly falls into it. But the important thing to remark is, that this Calvinism, which with the Calvinist is primary, is with Paul secondary, or even less than secondary. What with Calvinists is their fundamental idea, the centre of their theology, is for Paul an idea added to his central ideas, and extraneous to them ; brought in incidentally, and due to the necessities of a bad mode of recommending and enforcing his thesis. It is as if Newton had introduced into his exposition of the law of gravitation an incidental remark, perhaps erroneous, about light or colours ; and we were then to make this remark the head and front of Newton's law. The theological idea of reprobation was an idea of Jewish theology as of ours, an idea familiar to Paul and a part of his training, an idea which probably he never consciously abandoned. But its complete secondariness in him is clearly established by other considerations than those which we have drawn from the place and manner of his introduction of it. The very phrase about the clay and the potter is not Paul's own; he does but repeat a stock theological figure. Isaiah had said: 'O Lord, we are the clay, and thou our potter, and we are all the work of thy hand.'[1] Jeremiah had said, in the Lord's name, to Israel: 'Behold, as the clay in the potter's hand, so are ye in mine hand, O house of Israel.'[2] And the son of Sirach comes yet nearer to Paul's very words: 'As the clay is in the potter's hand to fashion it at his pleasure, so man is in the hand of him that made him, to render to them as liketh him best.'[3] Is an original man's essential, characteristic idea, that which he adopts thus bodily from some one else? But take Paul's truly essential idea. 'We are buried with Christ through baptism into death, that like as he was raised up from the dead by the glory of the Father, even so we also shall walk in newness of life.'[4] Did Jeremiah say that? Is any one the author of it except Paul? Then there should Calvinism have looked for Paul's secret, and not in the commonplace about the potter and the vessels of wrath. A commonplace which is so entirely a commonplace to him, that he contradicts it even while he is Judaising; for in the very batch of chapters we are discussing he says: 'Whosoever shall call upon the name of the Lord shall be saved.'[5] Still more clear is, on this point, his real mind, when he is not Judaising: 'God is the saviour of all men, specially of those that believe.'[6] And anything, finally, which might seem dangerous in the grateful sense of a calling, choosing,

[1] Is., lxiv, 8.
[2] Jer., xviii, 6.
[3] Ecclesiasticus, xxxiii, 13.
[4] Rom., vi, 4.
[5] Rom., x, 13.
[6] 1 Tim., iv, 10.

and leading by eternal goodness,—a notion as natural as the Calvinistic doctrine of predestination is monstrous,—Paul abundantly corrects in more than one striking passage; as, for instance, in that incomparable third·chapter of the Philippians (from which, and from the sixth and eighth chapters of the Romans, Paul's whole theology, if all his other writings were lost, might be reconstructed), where he expresses his humble consciousness that the mystical resurrection which is his aim, glory, and salvation, he does not yet, and cannot, completely attain.

The grand doctrine, then, which Calvinistic Puritanism has gathered from Paul turns out to be a secondary notion of his, which he himself, too, has contradicted or corrected. But, at any rate, 'Christ meritoriously obtained eternal redemption for us.' 'If there be anything,' the quarterly organ of Puritanism has solemnly told us in its hundredth number, 'that human experience has made certain, it is that man can never outgrow his necessity for the great truths and provisions of the Incarnation and the sacrificial Atonement of the Divine Son of God.' God, his justice being satisfied by Christ's bearing according to compact our guilt and dying in our stead, is appeased and set free to exercise towards us his mercy, and to justify and sanctify us in consideration of Christ's righteousness imputed to us, if we give our hearty belief and consent to the satisfaction thus made. This hearty belief being given, 'we rest,' to use the consecrated expression already quoted, 'in the finished work of a Saviour.' This doctrine of imputed righteousness is now, as predestination formerly was, the favourite thesis of popular Protestant theology. And, like the doctrine of predestination, it professes to be specially derived from St. Paul.

But whoever has followed attentively the main line of St. Paul's theology, as we have tried to show it, will see at once that in St. Paul's essential ideas this popular notion of a substitution, and appeasement, and imputation of alien merit, has no place. Paul knows nothing of a sacrificial atonement; what Paul knows of is a reconciling sacrifice. The true substitution, for Paul, is not the substitution of Jesus Christ in man's stead as victim on the cross to God's offended justice; it is the substitution by which the believer, in his own person, repeats Jesus Christ's dying to sin. Paul says, in real truth, to our Puritans with their magical and mechanical salvation, just what he said to the men of circumcision: 'If I preach resting in the finished work of a Saviour, *why am I yet persecuted? why do I die daily? then is the stumbling-block of the cross annulled.*[1] That hard, that well-nigh impossible doctrine, that our whole course must be a crucifixion and a resurrection, even as Christ's whole course was a crucifixion and a resurrection, becomes superfluous. Yet this is my central doctrine.'

The notion of God as a magnified and non-natural man, appeased by a sacrifice and remitting in consideration of it his wrath against those who had offended him,—this notion of God, which science repels, was equally repelled, in spite of all that his nation, time, and training had in them to favour it, by the profound religious sense of Paul. In none of his epistles is the reconciling work of Christ really presented under this aspect. One great epistle there is, however, which does apparently present it under this aspect,— the Epistle to the Hebrews.

Paul's phraseology, and even the central idea which he conveys in that phraseology, were evidently well known to the writer of the Epistle to the Hebrews. Nay, if we merely sought to prove a thesis, rather than to ascertain the real bearing of the documents we canvass, we should have no difficulty in making it appear, by texts taken from the Epistle to the Hebrews, that the doctrine of this epistle, no

[1] *Gal.*, v, 2.

less than the doctrine of the Epistle to the Romans, differs entirely from the common doctrine of Puritanism. This, however, we shall by no means do; because it is our honest opinion that the popular doctrine of 'the sacrificial Atonement of the Divine Son of God' derives, if not a real, yet at any rate a strong apparent sanction from the Epistle to the Hebrews. Even supposing, what is probably true, that the popular doctrine is really the doctrine neither of the one epistle nor of the other, yet it must be confessed that while it is the reader's fault,—a fault due to his fixed prepossessions, and to his own want of penetration,—if he gets the popular doctrine out of the Epistle to the Romans, it is on the other hand the writer's fault and no longer the reader's, if out of the Epistle to the Hebrews he gets the popular doctrine. For the author of that epistle is, if not subjugated, yet at least preponderantly occupied by the idea of the Jewish system of sacrifices, and of the analogies to Jesus Christ's sacrifice which are furnished by that system.

If other proof were wanting, this alone would make it impossible that the Epistle to the Hebrews should be Paul's; and indeed, of all the epistles which bear his name, it is the only one which we may not, perhaps, in spite of the hesitation caused by grave difficulties, be finally content to leave in considerable part to him.[1] Luther's conjecture, which

[1] Considerations drawn from date, place, the use of single words and phrases, the development of a church organisation, the development of an ascetic system, are not enough to make us wholly take away certain epistles from St. Paul. The only decisive evidence, for this purpose, is that internal evidence furnished by the entire body of the thoughts and style of an epistle; and this evidence that Paul was not its author the Epistle to the Hebrews furnishes. From the like evidence, the Apocalypse is clearly shown to be not by the author of the fourth Gospel. This clear evidence against the tradition which assigns them to St. Paul, the Epistles to Timothy and Titus do not offer. As to these epistles, the genuine critic will indeed find it impossible to assign them, as a whole, to St. Paul. But not only are they written by an

ascribes to Apollos the Epistle to the Hebrews, derives corroboration from the one account of Apollos which we have; that 'he was an eloquent man and mighty in the Scriptures.' The Epistle to the Hebrews is just such a performance as might naturally have come from an eloquent man and mighty in the Scriptures; in whom the intelligence, and the powers of combining, type-finding, and expounding, somewhat dominated the religious perceptions. The Epistle to the Hebrews is full of beauty and power; and what may be called the exterior conduct of its argument is as able and satisfying as Paul's exterior conduct of his argument is generally embarrassed. Its details are full of what is edifying; but its apparent central conception of Christ's death, as a perfect sacrifice which consummated the imperfect sacrifices of the Jewish law, is a mere notion of the understanding, and is not a religious idea. Turn it which way we will, the notion of appeasement of an offended God by vicarious sacrifice, which the Epistle to the Hebrews apparently sanctions, will never truly speak to the religious sense, or bear fruit for true religion. It is no blame to Apollos if he was somewhat overpowered by this notion, for the whole world was full of it, up to his time, in his time, and since his time; and it has driven theologians before it like sheep. The wonder is, not that Apollos should have adopted it, but that Paul should have been enabled, through the incomparable power and energy of religious perception informing his intellectual perception, in reality to put it aside. Figures drawn from the dominant notion of sacrificial appeasement he used, for the notion has so saturated the imagination and language of humanity that its figures pass naturally and irresistibly into all our speech. Popular Puritanism consists of the apparent doctrine from the Epistle

excellent man, and in an excellent and large spirit; they abound, also, with what are probably actual words and phrases of St. Paul.

to the Hebrews, set forth with Paul's figures. But the doctrine itself Paul had really put aside, and had substituted for it a better.

The term *sacrifice*, in men's natural use of it, contains three notions: the notion of winning the favour or buying off the wrath of a powerful being by giving him something precious; the notion of parting with something naturally precious; and the notion of expiation, not now in the sense of buying off wrath or satisfying a claim, but of suffering in that wherein we have sinned. The first notion is, at bottom, merely superstitious, and belongs to the ignorant and fear-ridden childhood of humanity; it is the main element, however, in the Puritan conception of justification. The second notion explains itself; it is the main element in the Pauline conception of justification. Jesus parted with what, to men in general, is the most precious of things,—individual self and selfishness; he pleased not himself, obeyed the spirit of God, died to sin and to the law in our members, consummated upon the cross this death; here is Paul's essential notion of Christ's sacrifice.

The third notion may easily be misdealt with, but it has a profound truth; in Paul's conception of justification there is much of it. In some way or other, he who would 'cease from sin' must nearly always 'suffer in the flesh.' It is found to be true, that 'without shedding of blood is no remission.' 'If you can be good with pleasure,' says Bishop Wilson with his genius of practical religious sense, 'God does not envy you your joy; but such is our corruption, that every man cannot be so.' The substantial basis of the notion of expiation, so far as we ourselves are concerned, is the bitter experience that the habit of wrong, of blindly obeying selfish impulse, so affects our temper and powers, that to withstand selfish impulse, to do right, when the sense of right awakens in us. requires an effort out of all proportion to the actual present emergency. We have not only the difficulty of the present act in itself, we have the resistance of all our past; fire and the knife, cautery and amputation, are often necessary in order to induce a vital action, which, if it were not for our corrupting past, we might have obtained from the natural healthful vigour of our moral organs. This is the real basis of our personal sense of the need of expiating, and thus it is that man expiates.

Not so the just, who is man's ideal. He has no indurated habit of wrong, no perverse temper, no enfeebled powers, no resisting past, no spiritual organs gangrened, no need of the knife and fire; smoothly and inevitably he follows the eternal order, and hereto belongs happiness What sins, then, has the just to expiate? *ours.* In truth, men's habitual unrighteousness, their hard and careless breaking of the moral law, do so tend to reduce and impair the standard of goodness, that, in order to keep this standard pure and unimpaired, the righteous must actually labour and suffer far more than would be necessary if men were better. In the first place, he has to undergo our hatred and persecution for his justice. In the second place, he has to make up for the harm caused by our continual shortcomings, to step between us foolish transgressors and the destructive natural consequences of our transgression, and, by a superhuman example, a spending himself without stint, a more than mortal scale of justice and purity, to save the ideal of human life and conduct from the deterioration with which men's ordinary practice threatens it. In this way Jesus Christ truly 'became for our sakes poor, though he was rich,' he was truly 'bruised for our iniquities,' he 'suffered in our behoof,' 'bare the sin of many,' and 'made intercession for the transgressors.'[1] In this way, truly, 'he was sacrificed as a blameless lamb to redeem us from the vain conversa-

[1] II *Cor.*, viii, 9; Is., liii, 5; I Pet., ii, 21; Is., liii, 12.

tion which had become our second nature ;'[1] in this way, 'he was made to be sin for us, who knew no sin.'[2] Such, according to that true and profound perception of the import of Christ's sufferings, which, in all St. Paul's writings, and in the inestimable First Epistle of St. Peter, is presented to us, is the expiation of Christ.

The notion, therefore, of *satisfying and appeasing an angry God's wrath*, does not come into Paul's real conception of Jesus Christ's sacrifice. Paul's foremost notion of this sacrifice is, that by it Jesus died to the law of selfish impulse, parted with what to men in general is most precious and near. Paul's second notion is, that whereas Jesus suffered in doing this, his suffering was not *his* need, but ours; not for *his* good, but for ours. In the first aspect, Jesus is the *martyrion*,—the testimony in his life and in his death, to righteousness, to the power and goodness of God. In the second aspect he is the *antilytron* or ransom. But, in either aspect, Jesus Christ's solemn and dolorous condemnation of sin does actually loosen sin's hold and attraction upon us who regard him,—makes it easier for us to understand and love goodness, to rise above self, to appropriate Christ, to die to sin.

Christ's sacrifice, however, and the condemnation of sin it contained, was made for us while we were yet sinners; it was made irrespectively of our power or inclination to sympathise with it and appreciate it. Yet, even thus, in Paul's view, the sacrifice reconciled us to God, to the eternal order; for it contained the means, the only possible means, of our being brought into harmony with this order. Jesus Christ, nevertheless, was delivered for our sins while we were yet sinners,[3] and before we could yet appreciate what he did. But presently there comes a change. Grace, the goodness of God, *the spirit*,—as Paul loved to call that awful and

[1] 1 Pet., i, 18, 19.   [2] II *Cor.*, v, 21.   [3] *Rom.*, v, 8.

beneficent impulsion of things within us and without us, which we can concur with, indeed, but cannot create,—leads us to *repentance towards God*,[1] a change of the inner man in regard to the moral order, duty, righteousness.[1] And now, to help this our impulse towards righteousness, we find a power enabling us to turn the impulse to full account. Now *the spirit* does its greatest work in us; because now, for the first time, the influence of Jesus Christ's pregnant act really gains us. For now awakens the sympathy for the act and the appreciation of it, which its doer dispensed with or was too benign to wait for; *faith working through love towards Christ*[2] enters into us, masters us. We *put on Christ*; we identify ourselves,—this is the line of Paul's thought,—with Christ; we repeat, through the power of this identification, Christ's death to the law of the flesh and self-pleasing, his condemnation of sin in the flesh; the death how imperfectly, the condemnation how remorsefully! But we also rise with him, Paul continues, to life, the only true life, of imitation of God, of putting on the new man which after God is created in righteousness and true holiness,[3] of following the eternal law of the moral order which by ourselves we could not follow. Then God justifies us. We have the righteousness of God and the sense of having it; we are freed from the oppressing sense of eternal order guiltily outraged and sternly retributive; we act in joyful conformity with God's will, instead of in miserable rebellion to it; we are in harmony with the universal order, and feel that we are in harmony with it. If, then, Christ was delivered for our sins, he was raised for our justification. If by Christ's death, says Paul, we were reconciled to God, by the means being thus provided for our else impossible access to God, much more, when we have availed ourselves of these means and died with him,

[1] *Acts*, xx, 21. [2] *Gal.*, v, 6. [3] *Eph.*, iv, 24.

are we saved by his life which we partake.¹ Henceforward we are not only justified but sanctified; not only in harmony with the eternal order and at peace with God, but consecrated² and unalterably devoted to them; and from this devotion comes an ever-growing union with God in Christ, an advance, as St. Paul says, from glory to glory.³

This is Paul's conception of Christ's sacrifice. His figures of ransom, redemption, propitiation, blood, offering, all subordinate themselves to his central idea of *identification with Christ through dying with him*, and are strictly subservient to it. The figured speech of Paul has its own beauty and propriety. His language is, much of it, eastern language, imaginative language; there is no need for turning it, as Puritanism has done, into the positive language of the schools. But if it is to be turned into positive language, then it is the language into which we have translated it that translates it truly.

We have before seen how it fares with one of the two great tenets which Puritanism has extracted from St. Paul, the tenet of predestination. We now see how it fares with the other, the tenet of justification. Paul's figures our Puritans have taken literally, while for his central idea they have substituted another which is not his. And his central idea they have turned into a figure, and have let it almost disappear out of their mind. His essential idea lost, his figures misused, an idea essentially not his substituted for his,—the unedifying patchwork thus made, Puritanism has stamped with Paul's name, and called *the gospel*. It thunders

---
[1] *Rom.*, v, 10.
[2] The endless words which Puritanism has wasted upon *sanctification*, a magical filling with goodness and holiness, flow from a mere mistake in translating; ἁγιασμός means *consecration*, a setting apart to holy service.
[3] II *Cor.*, iii, 18.

at Romanism for not preaching it, it casts off Anglicanism for not setting it forth alone and unreservedly, it founds organisations of its own to give full effect to it; these organisations guide politics, govern statesmen, destroy institutions; —and they are based upon a blunder!

It is to Protestantism, and this its Puritan gospel, that the reproaches thrown on St. Paul, for sophisticating religion of the heart into theories of the head about election and justification, rightly attach. St. Paul himself, as we have seen, begins with seeking righteousness and ends with finding it; from first to last, the practical religious sense never deserts him. If he could have seen and heard our preachers of predestination and justification, they are just the people he would have called 'diseased about questions and word-battlings.'[1] He would have told Puritanism that every Sunday, when in all its countless chapels it reads him and preaches from him, the veil is upon its heart. The moment it reads him right, a veil will seem to be taken away from its heart;[2] it will feel as though scales had fallen from its eyes.

But, leaving Puritanism and its errors, let us return, before we end, to the glorious apostle who has occupied us so long. He died, and men's familiar fancies of bargain and appeasement, from which, by a prodigy of religious insight, Paul had been able to disengage the death of Jesus, fastened on it and made it their own. Back rolled over the human soul the mist which the fires of Paul's spiritual genius had dispersed for a few short years. The mind of the whole world was imbrued in the idea of blood, and only through the false idea of sacrifice did men reach Paul's true one. Paul's idea of dying with Christ the *Imitation*

[1] 1 *Tim.*, vi, 4. [2] II *Cor.*, iii, 15, 16.

elevates more conspicuously than any Protestant treatise elevates it; but it elevates it environed and dominated by the idea of appeasement;—the magnified and non-natural man in Heaven, wrath-filled and blood-exacting; the human victim adding his piacular sufferings to those of the divine. Meanwhile another danger was preparing. Gifted men had brought to the study of St. Paul the habits of the Greek and Roman schools, and philosophised where Paul Orientalised. Augustine, a great genius, who can doubt it?—nay, a great religious genius, but unlike Paul in this, and inferior to him, that he confused the boundaries of metaphysics and religion, which Paul never did,—Augustine set the example of finding in Paul's eastern speech, just as it stood, the formal propositions of western dialectics. Last came the interpreter in whose slowly relaxing grasp we still lie,—the heavy-handed Protestant Philistine. Sincere, gross of perception, prosaic, he saw in Paul's mystical idea of man's investiture with the righteousness of God nothing but a strict legal transaction, and reserved all his imagination for Hell and the New Jerusalem. A so-called Pauline doctrine was in all men's mouths, but the ideas of the true Paul lay lost and buried.

Every one who has been at Rome has been taken to see the Church of St. Paul, rebuilt after a destruction by fire fifty years ago. The church stands a mile or two out of the city, on the way to Ostia and the desert. The interior has all the costly magnificence of Italian churches; on the ceiling is written in gilded letters: '*Doctor Gentium.*' Gold glitters and marbles gleam, but man and his movement are not there. The traveller has left at a distance the *fumum et opes strepitumque Romæ*; around him reigns solitude. There is Paul, alone with the mystery which was hidden from ages and from generations, which was brought to the light by him for some half score years, and which then was buried with him in his grave! Not in our day will he relive, with his incessant effort to find a moral side for miracle, with his incessant effort to make the intellect follow and secure all the workings of the religious perception. Of those who care for religion, the multitude of us want the materialism of the Apocalypse; the few want a vague religiosity. Science, which more and more teaches us to find in the unapparent the real, will gradually serve to conquer the materialism of popular religion. The friends of vague religiosity, on the other hand, will be more and more taught by experience that a theology, a scientific appreciation of the facts of religion, is wanted for religion; but a theology which is a true theology, not a false. Both these influences will work for Paul's re-emergence. The doctrine of Paul will arise out of the tomb where for centuries it has lain buried; it will edify the church of the future. It will have the consent of happier generations, the applause of less superstitious ages. All will be too little to pay half the debt which the church of God owes to this 'least of the apostles, who was not fit to be called an apostle, because he persecuted the church of God.'[1]

[1] 1 *Cor.*, xv, 9.

PURITANISM

AND THE

CHURCH OF ENGLAND.

In the foregoing treatise we have spoken of Protestantism, and have tried to show, how, with its three notable tenets of predestination, original sin, and justification, it has been pounding away for three centuries at St. Paul's wrong words, and missing his essential doctrine. And we took Puritanism to stand for Protestantism, and addressed ourselves directly to the Puritans; for the Puritan Churches, we said, seem to exist specially for the sake of these doctrines, one or more of them. It is true, many Puritans now profess also the doctrine that it is wicked to have a church connected with the State; but this is a later invention,[1] designed to strengthen a separation previously made. It requires to be noticed in due course; but meanwhile, we say that the aim of setting forth certain Protestant doctrines purely and integrally is the main title on which Puritan Churches rest their right of existing. With historic Churches, like those

[1] In his very interesting history, *The Church of the Restoration*, Dr. Stoughton says most truly of both Anglicans and Puritans in 1660: 'It is necessary to bear in mind this circumstance, that *both parties were advocates for a national establishment of religion.*' Vol. i, p. 113.

of England or Rome, it is otherwise ; these doctrines may
be in them, may be a part of their traditions, their theological
stock ; but certainly no one will say that either of these
Churches was made for the express purpose of upholding
these three theological doctrines, jointly or severally. A
little consideration will show quite clearly the difference in
this respect between the historic Churches and the churches
of separatists.

People are not necessarily monarchists or republicans
because they are born and live under a monarchy or republic.
They avail themselves of the established government for those
general purposes for which governments and politics exist,
but they do not, for the most part, trouble their heads much
about particular theoretical principles of government. Nay,
it may well happen that a man who lives and thrives under
a monarchy shall yet theoretically disapprove the principle
of monarchy, or a man who lives and thrives under a republic, the principle of republicanism. But a man, or body
of men, who have gone out of an established polity from
zeal for the principle of either monarchy or republicanism,
and have set up a polity of their own for the very purpose of
giving satisfaction to this zeal, are in a false position whenever it shall appear that the principle, from zeal for which
they have constituted their separate existence, is unsound.
So predestinarianism and solifidianism, Calvinism and
Lutherism, may appear in the theology of a national or historic Church, charged ever since the rise of Christianity
with the task of developing the immense and complex store
of ideas contained in Christianity ; and yet when the stage
of development has been reached at which the unsoundness
of predestinarian and solifidian dogmas becomes manifest,
they will be dropped out of the Church's theology, and she
and her task will remain what they were before. But when
people from zeal for these dogmas find their historic Church

not predestinarian or solifidian enough for them, and make new associations of their own which shall be predestinarian or solifidian absolutely, then, when the dogmas are undermined, the associations are undermined too, and have either to own themselves without a reason for existing, or to discover some new reason in place of the old. Now, nothing which exists likes to be driven to a strait of this kind; so every association which exists because of zeal for the dogmas of election or justification, will naturally cling to these dogmas longer and harder than other people. Therefore we have treated the Puritan bodies in this country as the great stronghold here of these doctrines; and in showing what a perversion of Paul's real ideas these doctrines commonly called Pauline are, we have addressed ourselves to the Puritans.

But those who speak in the Puritans' name say that we charge upon Puritanism, as a sectarian peculiarity, doctrine which is not only the inevitable result of an honest interpretation of the writings of St. Paul, but which is, besides, the creed held in common by Puritans and by all the churches in Christendom, with one insignificant exception. Nay, they even declare that 'no man in his senses can deny that the Church of England was meant to be a thoroughly Protestant and Evangelical, and it may be said Calvinistic Church.' To saddle Puritanism in special with the doctrines we have called Puritan is, they say, a piece of unfairness which has its motive in mere ill-will to Puritanism, a device which can injure nobody but its author.

Now, we have tried to show that the Puritans are quite wrong in imagining their doctrine to be the inevitable result of an honest interpretation of St. Paul's writings. That they are wrong we think is certain; but so far are we from being moved, in anything that we do or say in this matter, by ill-will to Puritanism and the Puritans, that it is on the contrary just because of our hearty respect for them, and from our strong sense of their value, that we speak as we do. Certainly we consider them to be in the main, at present, an obstacle to progress and to true civilisation. But this is because their worth is, in our opinion, such that not only must one for their own sakes wish to see it turned to more advantage, but others, from whom they are now separated, would greatly gain by conjunction with them, and our whole collective force of growth and progress be thereby immeasurably increased. In short, my one feeling when I regard them, is a feeling, not of ill-will, but of regret at waste of power; my one desire is a desire of comprehension.

But the waste of power must continue, and the comprehension is impossible, so long as Puritanism imagines itself to possess, in its two or three signal doctrines, what it calls *the gospel*; so long as it constitutes itself separately on the plea of setting forth purely *the gospel*, which it thus imagines itself to have seized; so long as it judges others as not holding *the gospel*, or as holding additions to it and variations from it. This fatal self-righteousness, grounded on a false conceit of knowledge, makes comprehension impossible; because it takes for granted the possession of the truth, and the power of deciding how others violate it; and this is a position of superiority, and suits conquest rather than comprehension.

The waste of power from not including the Puritans in the national Church is measured by the number and value of elements which Puritanism could supply towards the collective growth of the whole body. The national Church would grow more vigorously towards a higher stage of insight into religious truth, and consequently towards a greater perfection of practice, if it had these elements; and this is why we wish for the Puritans in the Church. But, Puritanism has refused to contribute to the common growth, mainly because it believes that a certain set of opinions or scheme of theological doctrine is *the gospel*; that it is possible and profitable to extract this, and that Puritans have done so; and that it is the duty of men, who like themselves have extracted it, to separate themselves from those who have not, and to set themselves apart that they may profess it purely.

To disabuse them of this error, which, by preventing collective life, prevents also collective growth, it is necessary to show them that their extracted scheme of theological doctrine is not really *the gospel*; and that at any rate, therefore, it is not worth their while to separate themselves, and to frustrate the hope of growth in common, merely for this scheme's sake. And even if it were true, as they allege, that the national and historic Churches of Christendom do equally with Puritanism hold this scheme, or main parts of it, still it would be to Puritanism, and not to the historic Churches, that in showing the invalidity and unscripturalness of this scheme we should address ourselves, because the Puritan Churches found their very existence on it, and the historic Churches do not. And not founding their existence on it, nor falling into separatism for it, the historic Churches have a collective life which is very considerable, and a power of growth, even in respect of the very scheme of doctrine in question, supposing them to hold it, far greater than any which the Puritan Churches show, but which would be yet greater and more fruitful still, if the historic Churches combined the large and admirable contingent of Puritanism with their own forces. Therefore, as we have said, it is out of no sort of malice or ill-will, but from esteem for their fine qualities and from desire for their help, that we have addressed ourselves to the Puritans. We propose to complete now our dealings with this subject by showing how, as a matter of fact, the Church of England (which is the historic Church practically in question so far as Puritanism is concerned) seems to us to have displayed with respect to those very tenets which we have criticised, and for which we are said to have unfairly made Puritanism alone responsible, a continual power of growth which has been wanting to the Puritan congregations. This we propose to show first; and we will show secondly, how, from the very theory of a historic or national Church, the probability of this greater power of growth seems to follow, that we may try and commend that theory a little more to the thoughts and favour of our Puritan friends.

The two great Puritan doctrines which we have criticised at such length are the doctrines of predestination and justification. Of the aggressive and militant Puritanism of our people, predestination has, almost up to the present day, been the favourite and distinguishing doctrine; it was the doctrine which Puritan flocks greedily sought, which Puritan ministers powerfully preached, and called others *carnal gospellers* for not preaching. This Geneva doctrine accompanied the Geneva discipline. Puritanism's first great wish and endeavour was to establish both the one and the other absolutely in the Church of England, and it became nonconforming because it failed. Now, it is well known that the High Church divines of the seventeenth century were Arminian, that the Church of England was the stronghold of Arminianism, and that Arminianism is, as we have said, an effort of man's practical good sense to get rid of what is shocking to it in Calvinism. And eminently worthy of remark is the constant pressure applied by Puritanism upon the Church of England, to put the Calvinistic doctrine more distinctly into her formularies, and to tie her up more strictly to this doctrine; the constant resistance offered by the Church of England, and the large degree in which Nonconformity is really due to this cause.

Everybody knows how far Nonconformity is due to the Church of England's rigour in imposing an explicit declaration of adherence to her formularies. But only a few, who have searched out the matter, know how far Nonconformity is due, also, to the Church of England's invincible reluctance to narrow her large and loose formularies to the strict Calvinistic sense dear to Puritanism. Yet this is what the record of conferences shows at least as signally as it shows the domineering spirit of the High Church clergy; but our current political histories, written always with an anti-ecclesiastical bias, which is natural enough, inasmuch as the Church party was not the party of civil liberty, leaves this singularly out of sight. Yet there is a very catena of testimonies to prove it; to show us, from Elizabeth's reign to Charles the Second's, Calvinism, as a power both within and without the Church of England, trying to get decisive command of her formularies; and the Church of England, with the instinct of a body meant to live and grow, and averse to fetter and engage its future, steadily resisting.

The Lambeth Articles of 1595 exhibit Calvinism potent in the Church of England herself, and among the bishops of the Church. True; but could it establish itself there? No; the Lambeth Articles were recalled and suppressed, and Archbishop Whitgift was threatened with the penalties of a *præmunire* for having published them. Again, it was usual from 1552 onwards to print in the English Bibles a catechism asserting the Calvinistic doctrine of absolute election and reprobation. In the first Bibles of the authorised version this catechism appeared; but it was removed in 1615. Yet the Puritans had met James the First, at his accession in 1603, with the petition that *there may be an uniformity of doctrine prescribed*; meaning an uniformity in this sense of strict Calvinism. Thus from the very commencement the Church, as regards doctrine, was for opening; Puritanism was for narrowing.

Then came, in 1604, the Hampton Court Conference. Here, as usual, political historians reproach the Church with having conceded so little. These historians, as we have said, think solely of the Puritans as the religious party favourable to civil liberty, and on that account they favour Puritanism in its disputes with the Church. But, as regards freedom of thought and truth of ideas, what was it that the Church was pressed by Puritanism to concede, and what was the character and tendency of the Church's refusal? The first Puritan petition at this Conference was 'that the *doctrine* of the Church might be preserved in purity according to God's Word.' That is, according to the Calvinistic interpretation put upon God's Word by Calvin and the Puritans after him; an interpretation which we have shown to be erroneous and unscriptural. This Calvinistic doctrine of predestination the Puritans wanted to plant hard and fast in the Church's formularies, and the Church resisted. The Puritan foreman complained of the loose wording of the Thirty-nine Articles because it allowed an escape from the strict doctrine of Calvinism, and moved that the Lambeth Articles, strictly Calvinistic, might be inserted into the Book of Articles. The Bishops resisted, and here are the words of their spokesman, the Bishop of London. 'The Bishop of London answered, that too many in those days, neglecting holiness of life, *laid all their religion upon predestination*, —" If I shall be saved, I shall be saved," which he termed a desperate doctrine, showing it to be contrary to good divinity, which teaches us to reason rather *ascendendo* than *descendendo*, thus: " I live in obedience to God, in love with my neighbour, I follow my vocation, &c., therefore I trust that God hath elected me and predestinated me to salvation;" not thus, which is the usual course of argument: "God hath predestinated and chosen me to life, therefore, though I sin never so grievously, I shall not be damned, for whom he once loveth he loveth to the end."' Who will deny that this resistance of the Church to the Puritans, who, *laying all their religion upon predestination*, wanted to make the Church do the same, was as favourable to growth of thought and to sound philosophy, as it was consonant to good sense?

We have already, in the foregoing treatise, quoted from the complaints against the Church by the Committee of Divines appointed by the House of Lords in 1641, when Puritanism was strongly in the ascendant. Some in the Church teach, say the Puritan complainers, 'that good works are concauses with faith in the act of justification; some have oppugned the certitude of salvation; some have maintained that the Lord's day is kept merely by ecclesiastical constitution; some have defended the whole gross substance of Arminianism, that the act of conversion depends upon the concurrence of men's free will; some have denied original sin; some have broached out of Socinus a most uncomfortable and desperate doctrine, that late repentance, —that is, upon the last bed of sickness,—is unfruitful.' Such is the complaint; and what we insist upon is, that the growth and movement of thought, on religious matters, are here shown to be in the Church; and that on these two cardinal doctrines of predestination and justification, with which we are accused of unfairly saddling Puritanism alone, Puritanism did really want to make the national religion hinge while the Church did not, but resisted.

The resistance of the Church was at that time vanquished, not by importing strict Calvinism into the Prayer Book, but by casting out the Prayer Book altogether. By ordinance in 1645 the use of the Prayer Book, which for churches had already been forbidden, was forbidden also for all private places and families; any copies to be found in churches were to be delivered up, and heavy penalties were imposed on persons retaining them.

We come next to the occasion where the Church is thought to have most decisively shown her unyieldingness,—the Savoy Conference in 1661, after King Charles the Second's restoration. The question was, what alterations were to be made in the Prayer Book, so as to enable the Puritans to use it as well as the Church party. Having in view doctrine and free development of thought, we say again it was the Puritans who were for narrowing, it was the Churchmen who were for keeping open. Their heads full of these tenets of predestination, original sin, and justification, which we are accused of charging upon them exclusively and unfairly, the Puritans complain that the Church Liturgy seems very defective,—why? Because 'the systems of doctrine of a church should summarily comprehend all such doctrines as are necessary to be believed,' and the liturgy does not set down these explicitly enough. For instance, 'the Confession,' they say, 'is very defective, not clearly expressing original sin. The Catechism is defective as to many necessary doctrines of our religion, some even of the essentials of Christianity not being mentioned except in the Creed, and there not so explicit as ought to be in a catechism.' And what is the answer of the bishops? It is the answer of people with an instinct that this definition and explicitness demanded by the Puritans are incompatible with the conditions of life of a historic church. 'The Church,' they say, 'hath been careful to put nothing into the Liturgy but that which is either evidently the Word of God, or what hath been generally received in the Catholic Church. The Catechism is not intended as a whole body of divinity.' The Puritans had requested that 'the Church prayers might contain *nothing questioned by pious, learned, and orthodox per-*

sons.' Seizing on this expression, wherein is contained the ground of that *separatism for opinions* which we hold to be so fatal not only to Church life but also to the natural growth of religious thought, the bishops ask, and in the very language of good sense: 'Who are *pious, learned, and orthodox persons?* Are we to take for such all who shall confidently affirm themselves to be such? If by orthodox be meant those who adhere to Scripture and the Catholic consent of antiquity, we do not yet know that any part of our Liturgy has been questioned by such. It was the wisdom of our reformers to draw up *such a liturgy as neither Romanist nor Protestant could justly except against.* Persons want the book to be altered for their own satisfaction.'

This allegation of the bishops respecting the character of the Liturgy is undoubtedly true, for the Puritans themselves expressly admitted its truth, and urged this as a reason for altering the Liturgy. It is in consonance with what is so often said, and truly said, of the Thirty-nine Articles, that they are *articles of peace.* This, indeed, makes the Articles scientifically worthless. Metaphysical propositions, such as they in the main are, drawn up with a studied design for their being vague and loose, can have no metaphysical value. But no one then thought of doing without metaphysical articles; so to make them articles of peace showed a true conception of the conditions of life and growth in a church. The readiness to put a lax sense on subscription is a proof of the same disposition of mind. Chillingworth's judgment about the meaning of subscription is well known. 'For the Church of England, I am persuaded that the constant doctrine of it is so pure and orthodox, that whosoever believes it and lives according to it, undoubtedly he shall be saved; and that there is no error in it which may necessitate or warrant any man to disturb the peace or renounce the communion of it. *This in my opinion is all that is intended by subscription.*' And Laud, a very different man from Chillingworth, held on this point a like opinion with him.

Certainly the Church of England was in no humour, at the time of the Savoy Conference, to deal tenderly with the Puritans. It was too much disposed to show to the Puritans the same sort of tenderness which the Puritans had shown to the Church. The nation, moreover, was nearly as illdisposed as the Church to the Puritans; and this proves well what the narrowness and tyrannousness of Puritanism dominant had really been. But the Church undoubtedly said and did to Puritanism after the Restoration much that was harsh and bitter, and therefore inexcusable in a Christian church. Examples of Churchmen so speaking and dealing may be found in the transactions of 1661; but perhaps the most offensive example of a Churchman of this kind, and who deserves therefore to be studied, is a certain Dr. Jane, Regius Professor of Divinity at Oxford and Dean of Gloucester, who was put forward to thwart Tillotson's projects of comprehension in 1689. A certain number of Dr. Janes there have always been in the Church. There are a certain number of them in the Church now, and there always will be a certain number of them. No Church could exist with many of them; but one should have a sample or two of them always before one's mind, and remember how to the excluded party a few, and those the worst, of their excluders, are always apt to stand for the whole, in order to comprehend the full bitterness and resentment of Puritanism against the Church of England. Else one would be inclined to say, after attentively and impartially observing the two parties, that the persistence of the Church in pressing for conformity arose, not as the political historians have it, from the lust of haughty ecclesiastics for dominion and for imposing their law on the vanquished, but from a real sense that their formularies were made so large and open, and the sense put upon subscription to them was so indulgent, that any reasonable man could honestly conform; and that it was perverseness and determination to impose their special ideas on the Church, and to narrow the Church's latitude, which made the Puritans stand out.

Nay, and it was with the wording of the Prayer Book as it was with its doctrine; the Church took the side which most commands the sympathy of liberal-minded men. Baxter had his rival Prayer Book which he proposed to substitute for the old one. And this is how the 'Reformed Liturgy' was to begin: 'Eternal, incomprehensible and invisible God, infinite in power, wisdom and goodness, dwelling in the light which no man can approach, where thousand thousands minister unto thee, and ten thousand times ten thousand stand before thee,' &c. This, I say, was to have taken the place of our old friend, *Dearly beloved brethren*; and here, again, we can hardly refuse approval to the Church's resistance to Puritan innovations. We could wish, indeed, the Church had shown the same largeness in consenting to relax ceremonies, which she showed in refusing to tighten dogma, or to spoil diction. Worse still, the angry wish to drive by violence, when the other party will not move by reason, finally no doubt appears; and the Church has much to blame herself for in the Act of Uniformity. Blame she deserves, and she has had it plentifully; but what has not been enough perceived is, that really the conviction of her own moderation, openness, and latitude, as regards doctrine, seems to have filled her mind during her dealings with the Puritans; and that her impatience with them was in great measure impatience at seeing these so ill-appreciated by them. Very ill-appreciated by them they certainly were; and, as far as doctrine is concerned, the quarrel between the Church and Puritanism undoubtedly was, that for the doctrines of pedestination, original sin, and justification, Puritanism wanted more exclusive prominence, more dogmatic definition, more bar to future escape and development; while the Church resisted.

And as the instinct of the Church always made her avoid, on these three favourite tenets of Puritanism, the stringency of definition which Puritanism tried to force upon her, always made her leave herself room for growth in regard to them,—so, if we look for the positive beginnings and first signs of growth, of disengagement from the stock notions of popular theology about predestination, original sin, and justification, it is among Churchmen, and not among Puritans, that we shall find them. Few will deny that as to the doctrines of predestination and original sin, at any rate, the mind of religious men is no longer what it was in the seventeenth century or in the eighteenth. There has been evident growth and emancipation; Puritanism itself no longer holds these doctrines in the rigid way it once did. To whom is this change owing? who were the beginners of it? They were men using that comparative openness of mind and accessibility to ideas which was fostered by the Church. The very complaints which we have quoted from the Puritan divines prove that this was so. Henry More, saying in the heat of the Calvinistic controversy, what it needed insight to say then, but what almost every one's common sense says now, that 'it were to be wished the Quinquarticular points were all reduced to this one, namely, *That none shall be saved without sincere obedience*;' Jeremy Taylor saying in the teeth of the superstitious popular doctrine of original sin: 'Original sin, as it is at this day commonly explicated, was not the doctrine of the primitive church; but when Pelagius had puddled the stream, St. Austin was so angry that he stamped and puddled it more,' —this sort of utterance from Churchmen it was, that first introduced into our religious world the current of more independent thought concerning the doctrines of predestination and original sin, which has now made its way even amidst Puritans themselves.

Here the emancipation has reached the Puritans; but it proceeded from the Church. That Puritanism is yet emancipated from the popular doctrine of justification cannot be asserted. On the contrary, the more it loosens its hold on the doctrine of predestination the more it tightens it on that of justification. We shall have occasion by and by to discuss Wesley's words: '*Plead thou solely the blood of the Covenant, the ransom paid for thy proud stubborn soul!*' and to show how modern Methodism glories in holding aloft as its standard this teaching of Wesley's, and this teaching above all. The many tracts which have lately been sent me in reference to this subject go all the same way. Like Luther, they hold that 'all heretics have continually failed in this one point, that they do not rightly understand or know the article of *justification*:' 'do not see' (to continue to use Luther's words,) 'that by none other sacrifice or offering could God's fierce anger be appeased, but by the precious blood of the Son of God.' That this doctrine is founded upon an entire misunderstanding of St. Paul's writings we have shown; that there is now very visible a tendency in the minds of religious people to outgrow it, is true, but where alone does this tendency manifest itself with any steadiness or power? In the Church. The inevitable movement of growth will in time extend itself to Puritanism also. Let it be remembered in that day that not only does the movement come to Puritanism from the Church, but it comes to Churchmen of our century from a seed of growth and development inherent in the Church, and which was manifest in the Church long ago.

That the accompaniments of the doctrine of justification,—the tenets of conversion, instantaneous sanctification, assurance, and sinless perfection,—tenets which are not the essence of Wesley, but which are the essence of Wesleyan Methodism, and which have in them so much that is delusive and dangerous,—that these should have been discerningly judged by that mixture of piety and sobriety which marks Anglicans of the best type, such as Bishop Wilson,[1] will surprise no one. Years before Wesley was born, the fontal doctrine itself,—Wesley's '*Plead thou solely the blood of the Covenant!*'—had been criticised by Hammond thus, and the signal of deliverance from the Lutheran doctrine of justification given: 'The solifidian looks upon his faith as the utmost accomplishment and end, and not only as the first elements of his task, which is *the superstructing of good life*. The solifidian believes himself to have the only sanctified necessary doctrines, that having them renders his condition safe and every man who believes them a pure Christian professor. In respect of solifidianism it is worth remembering what Epiphanius observes of the primitive times, that *wickedness was the only heresy*, that impious and pious living divided the whole Christian world into erroneous and orthodox.'

In point of fact, therefore, the historic Church in England, not existing for special opinions but proceeding by development, has shown much greater freedom of mind as regards the doctrines of election, original sin, and justification, than the Nonconformists have; and has refused, in spite of Puritan pressure, to tie herself too strictly to these doctrines, to make them all in all. She thus both has been and is more serviceable than Puritanism to religious progress; because the separating for opinions, which is proper to Puritanism,

[1] For example, what an antidote to the perilous Methodist doctrine of instantaneous sanctification is this saying of Bishop Wilson: 'He who fancies that his mind may effectually be changed in a short time, deceives himself.'

rivets the separatist to those opinions, and is thus opposed to that development and gradual exhibiting of the full sense of the Bible and Christianity, which is essential to religious progress. To separate for the doctrine of predestination, of justification, of scriptural church-discipline, is to be false to the idea of development, to imagine that you can seize the absolute sense of Scripture from your own present point of view, and to cut yourself off from growth and gradual illumination. That a comparison between the course things have taken in Puritanism and in the Church goes to prove the truth of this as a matter of fact, is what I have been trying to show hitherto; in what follows I purpose to show how, as a matter of theory and antecedent likelihood, it seems probable and natural that so this should be.

A historic Church cannot choose but allow the principle of development, for it is written in its institutions and history. An admirable writer, in a book which is one of his least known works, but which contains, perhaps, even a greater number of profound and valuable ideas than any other one of them, has set forth, both persuasively and truly, the impression of this sort which Church-history cannot but convey. 'We have to account,' says Cardinal Newman in his *Essay on Development*, 'for that apparent variation and growth of doctrine which embarrasses us when we would consult history for the true idea of Christianity. The increase and expansion of the Christian creed and ritual, and the variations which have attended the process in the case of individual writers and churches, are the necessary attendants on any philosophy or polity which takes possession of the intellect and heart, and has had any wide or extended dominion. From the nature of the human mind, time is necessary for the full comprehension and perfection of great ideas. The highest and most wonderful truths, though communicated to the world once for all by inspired teachers, could not be comprehended all at once by the recipients; but, as admitted and transmitted by minds not inspired, and through media which were human, have required only the longer time and deeper thought for their full elucidation.' And again: 'Ideas may remain when the expression of them is indefinitely varied. Nay, one cause of corruption in religion is the refusal to follow the course of doctrine as it moves on, and an obstinacy in the notions of the past. So our Lord found his people precisians in their obedience to the letter; he condemned them for not being led on to its spirit,—that is, its development. The Gospel is the development of the Law; yet what difference seems wider than that which separates the unbending rule of Moses from the grace and truth which came by Jesus Christ? The more claim an idea has to be considered living, the more various will be its aspects; and the more social and political is its nature, the more complicated and subtle will be its developments, and the longer and more eventful will be its course. Such is Christianity.' And yet once more: 'It may be objected that inspired documents, such as the Holy Scriptures, at once determine doctrine without further trouble. But they were intended to create *an idea*, and that idea is not in the sacred text, but in the mind of the reader; and the question is, whether that idea is communicated to him in its completeness and minute accuracy on its first apprehension, or expands in his heart and intellect, and comes to perfection in the course of time. If it is said that inspiration supplied the place of this development in the first recipients of Christianity, still the time at length came when its recipients ceased to be inspired; and on these recipients the revealed truths would fall as in other cases, at first vaguely and generally, and would afterwards be completed by developments.'

The notion thus admirably expounded of a gradual

understanding of the Bible, a progressive development of Christianity, is the same which was in Bishop Butler's mind when he laid down in his *Analogy* that 'the Bible contains many truths as yet undiscovered.' 'And as,' he says, 'the whole scheme of Scripture is not yet understood, so, if it ever comes to be understood, before the restitution of all things and without miraculous interpositions, it must be in the same way as natural knowledge is come at,—by the continuance and progress of learning and of liberty, and by particular persons attending to, comparing, and pursuing intimations scattered up and down it, which are overlooked and disregarded by the generality of the world. For this is the way in which all improvements are made; by thoughtful men's tracing on obscure hints, as it were, dropped as by nature accidentally, or which seem to come into our minds by chance.' And again : 'Our existence is not only successive, as it must be of necessity, but one state of our life and being is appointed by God to be a preparation for another, and that to be the means of attaining to another succeeding one; infancy to childhood, childhood to youth, youth to mature age. Men are impatient and for precipitating things ; but the author of nature appears deliberate throughout his operations, accomplishing his natural ends by slow successive steps. Thus, in the daily course of natural providence, God operates in the very same manner as in the dispensation of Christianity; making one thing subservient to another, this to somewhat further; and so on, through a progressive series of means which extend both backward and forward beyond our utmost view. Of this manner of operation everything we see in the course of nature is as much an instance as any part of the Christian dispensation.'

All this is indeed incomparably well said; and with Cardinal Newman we may, on the strength of it all, beyond any doubt 'fairly conclude that Christian doctrine admits of developments;' that 'the whole Bible is written on the principle of development.'

Cardinal Newman, indeed, uses this idea in a manner which, though ingenious, seems to us arbitrary and condemned by the idea itself. He uses it in support of the pretensions of the Church of Rome to an infallible authority on points of doctrine. He says, with much ingenuity, to Protestants: The doctrines you receive are no more on the face of the Bible, or in the plain teaching of the ante-Nicene Church, which alone you consider pure, than the doctrines you reject. The doctrine of the Trinity is a development, as much as the doctrine of Purgatory. Both of them are developments made by the Church, by the post-Nicene Church. The determination of the Canon of Scripture, a thing of vital importance to you who acknowledge no authority but Scripture, is a development due to the post-Nicene Church.—And thus Dr. Newman would compel Protestants to admit that which is, he declares, in itself reasonable,—namely, 'the probability of the appointment in Christianity of an external authority to decide upon the true developments of doctrine and practice in it, thereby separating them from the mass of mere human speculation, extravagance, corruption, and error, in and out of which they grow. This is the doctrine of the infallibility of the Church, of faith and obedience towards the Church, founded on the probability of its never erring in its declarations or commands.'

Now, asserted in this absolute way, and extended to doctrine as well as discipline, to speculative thought as well as to Christian practice, Dr. Newman's conclusion seems at variance with his own theory of development, and to be something like an instance of what Bishop Butler criticises when he says: 'Men are impatient, and for precipitating things.' But Dr. Newman has himself supplied us with a sort of commentary on these words of Butler's which is worth quoting, because it throws more light on our point than Butler's few words can throw on it by themselves. Dr. Newman says : 'Development is not an effect of wishing and resolving, or of forced enthusiasm, or of any mechanism of reasoning, or of any mere subtlety of intellect; but comes of its own innate power of expansion within the mind in its season, though with the use of reflexion and argument and original thought, more or less as it may happen, with a dependence on the ethical growth of the mind itself, and with a reflex influence upon it.'

It is impossible to point out more sagaciously and expressively the natural, spontaneous, free character of true development; how such a development must follow laws of its own, may often require vast periods of time, cannot be hurried, cannot be stopped. And so far as Christianity deals,—as, in its metaphysical theology, it does abundantly deal,—with thought and speculation, it must surely be admitted that for its true and ultimate development in this line more time is required, and other conditions have to be fulfilled, than we have had already. So far as Christian doctrine contains speculative philosophical ideas, never since its origin have the conditions been present for determining these adequately; certainly not in the mediæval Church, which so dauntlessly strove to determine them. And therefore on every Creed and Council is judgment passed in Bishop Butler's sentence : '*The Bible contains many truths as yet undiscovered.*'

The Christian religion has practice for its great end and aim ; but it raises, as anyone can see, and as Church-history proves, numerous and great questions of philosophy and of scientific criticism. Well, for the true elucidation of such questions, and for their final solution, time and favourable developing conditions are confessedly necessary. From the end of the apostolic age and of the great fontal burst of Christianity, down to the present time, have such conditions ever existed in the Christian communities, for determining adequately the questions of philosophy and scientific criticism which the Christian religion raises? *God, creation, will, evil, atonement, immortality,*—these terms and many more of the same kind, however much they might in the Bible be used in a concrete and practical manner, yet plainly had in themselves a provocation to abstract thought, carried with them the occasions of a criticism and a philosophy, which must sooner or later make its appearance in the Church. It did make its appearance; and the question is whether it has ever yet appeared there under conditions favourable to its true development. Surely this is best elucidated by considering whether questions of criticism and philosophy in general ever had one of their happy moments, their times for successful development, in the early and middle ages of Christendom at all, or have had one of them in the Christian churches, as such, since. All these questions hang together, and the time that is improper for solving one sort of them rightly is improper also for solving the others.

Surely, then, historic criticism, criticism of style, criticism of nature, no one would go to the early or middle ages of the Church for illumination on these matters. How, therefore, should those ages develop successfully a philosophy of theology, or, in other words, a criticism of physics and metaphysics, which involves the three other criticisms and more besides? Church-theology is an elaborate attempt at a philosophy of theology, at a philosophical criticism. In Greece, before Christianity appeared, there had been a favouring period for the development of such a criticism; a considerable movement of it took place, and considerable results were reached. When Christianity began, this movement was in decadence; it declined more and more till it died quite out; it revived very slowly, and as it waxed, the mediæval Church waned. The doctrine of universals is a question of philosophy discussed in Greece, and re-discussed in the middle ages. Whatever light this doctrine receives from Plato's treatment of it, or Aristotle's, in whatever state they left it, will anyone say that the Nominalists and Realists brought any more light to it, that they developed it in any way, or could develop it? For the same reason, St. Augustine's criticism of God's eternal decrees, original sin, and justification, the criticism of St. Thomas Aquinas on them, the decisions of the Church on them, are of necessity, and from the very nature of things, inadequate, because, being philosophical developments, they are made in an age when the forces for true philosophical development are waning or wanting.

So when Hooker says most truly: 'Our belief in the Trinity, the co-eternity of the Son of God with his Father, the proceeding of the Spirit from the Father and the Son, with other principal points the necessity whereof is by none denied, are notwithstanding in Scripture nowhere to be found by express literal mention, only deduced they are out of Scripture by collection;'—when Hooker thus points out, what is undoubtedly the truth, that these Church-doctrines are developments, we may add this other truth equally undoubted,—that being *philosophical* developments, they are developments of a kind which the Church has never yet had the right conditions for making adequately, any more than it has had the conditions for developing out of what is said in the book of Genesis, a true philosophy of nature, or out of what is said in the Book of Daniel, a true philosophy of history. It matters nothing whether the scientific truth was there, and the problem was to extract it: or not there, and the problem was to understand why it was not there, and the relation borne by what *was* there to the scientific truth. The

Church had no means of solving either the one problem or the other. And this from no fault at all of the Church, but for the same reason that she was unfitted to solve a difficulty in Aristotle's *Physics* or Plato's *Timæus*, and to determine the historical value of Herodotus or Livy; simply from the natural operation of the law of development, which for success in philosophy and criticism requires certain conditions that in the early and mediæval Church were not to be found.

And when the movement of philosophy and criticism came with the Renascence, this movement was almost entirely outside the Churches, whether Catholic or Protestant, and not inside them. It worked in men like Descartes and Bacon, and not in men like Luther and Calvin; so that the doctrine of these two eminent personages, Luther and Calvin, so far as it was a philosophical and critical development from Scripture, had no more likelihood of being an adequate development than the doctrine of the Council of Trent. And so it has gone on to this day. Philosophy and criticism have become a great power in the world, and inevitably tend to alter and develop Church-doctrine, so far as this doctrine is, as to a great extent it is, philosophical and critical. Yet the seat of the developing force is not in the Church itself, but elsewhere; its influences filter strugglingly into the Church, and the Church slowly absorbs and incorporates them. And whatever hinders their filtering in and becoming incorporated, hinders truth and the natural progress of things.

While, therefore, we entirely agree with Dr. Newman and with the great Anglican divines that the whole Bible is written on the principle of development, and that Christianity in its doctrine and discipline is and must be a development of the Bible, we yet cannot agree that for the adequate development of Christian doctrine, so far as theology exhibits this metaphysically and scientifically, the Church, whether ante-Nicene or post-Nicene, has ever yet furnished a channel. Thought and science follow their own law of development, they are slowly elaborated in the growth and forward pressure of humanity, in what Shakespeare calls—

. . . . the prophetic soul
Of the wide world dreaming on things to come;

and their ripeness and unripeness, as Dr. Newman most truly says, are not an effect of our wishing or resolving. Rather do they seem brought about by a power such as Goethe figures by the *Zeit-Geist* or Time-Spirit, and St. Paul describes as a divine power *revealing* additions to what we possess already.

But sects of men are apt to be shut up in sectarian ideas of their own, and to be less open to new general ideas than the main body of men; therefore St. Paul in the same breath exhorts to unity. What may justly be conceded to the Catholic Church is, that in her idea of a continuous developing power in united Christendom to work upon the data furnished by the Bible, and produce new combinations from them as the growth of time required it, she followed a true instinct. But the right *philosophical* developments she vainly imagined herself to have had the power to produce, and her attempts in this direction were at most but a prophecy of this power, as alchemy is said to have been a prophecy of chemistry.

Still, essentially the Church was not a corporation for speculative purposes, but a corporation for purposes of moral growth and of practice. Terms like *God, creation, will, evil, atonement, immortality*, evoke, as we have said, and must evoke, sooner or later, a philosophy; but to evoke this was the accident and not the essence of Christianity? What, then, was the essence?

Sir James Stephen, a writer as unlike Dr. Newman as it

is possible to conceive, has told us. In an article in *Fraser's Magazine*,—an article written with great vigour and acuteness,—this writer advises us to return to Paley, whom we were beginning to neglect, because the real important essence, he says, of Christianity, or rather, to quote quite literally, 'the only form of Christianity which is worthy of the serious consideration of rational men, is Protestantism as stated by Paley and his school.' And why? 'Because this Protestantism enables the saint to prove to the worldly man that Christ threatened him with hell-fire, and proved his power to threaten by rising from the dead and ascending into heaven : *and these allegations are the fundamental assertions of Christianity.*'

Now it may be said that this is a very contracted view of 'the unsearchable riches of Christ ;' but we will not quarrel with it. And this for several reasons. In the first place, it is the view often taken by popular theology. In the second place, it is the view best fitted to serve its Benthamite author's object, which is to get Christianity out of the way altogether. In the third place, its shortness gives us courage to try and do what is the hardest thing in the world, namely, to pack a statement of the main drift of Christianity into a few lines of nearly as short compass.

What then was, in brief, the Christian gospel, or 'good news'? It was this : *The kingdom of God is come unto you!* The power of Jesus upon the multitudes who heard him gladly was not that, by rising from the dead and ascending into heaven, he enabled the saint to prove to the worldly man the certainty of hell-fire (for he had not yet done so), but that *he talked to them about the kingdom of God.*[1] And

---

[1] Nothing can be more certain than that the *kingdom of God* meant originally, and was understood to mean, a Messianic kingdom speedily to appear ; and that to this idea of the *kingdom* is due much of the effect which its preaching exercised on the imagination of the first

how was this come to mankind? Because *Jesus is come to save his people from their sins.* And how does Jesus save us from our sins? By teaching us *to take his yoke upon us, to do God's will, and to lose our life for the purpose of saving it.*

On this foundation arose the Christian Church, and not on any foundation of speculative metaphysics. It was inevitable that the speculative metaphysics should come, but they were not the foundation. When they came, the danger of the Christian Church was that she should take them for the foundation. The Christians who were built on the real foundation, who were united in the joy of Christ's good news, naturally, as they came to know of one another's existence, as their relations with one another multiplied, as the sense of sympathy in the possession of a common treasure deepened,—naturally, I say, drew together in one body, with an organisation growing out of the needs of a growing body. It is quite clear that the more strongly Christians felt their common business in setting forward upon earth, through Christ's spirit, the kingdom of God, the more they would be drawn to coalesce into one society for this business, with the natural and true notion that the acting together in this way offers to men greater helps for

generation of Christians. But nothing is more certain, also, than that while the end itself, the Messianic kingdom, was necessarily something intangible and future, the *way* to the end, the doing the will of God by intently following the voice of the moral conscience, in those duties, above all, for which there was then in the world the most crying need,—the duties of humbleness, self-denial, pureness, justice, charity,—became from the very first in the teaching of Jesus something so ever-present and practical, and so associated with the essence of Jesus himself, that the *way* to the kingdom grew inseparable, in thought, from the kingdom itself, and was bathed in the same light and charm. Then, after a time, as the vision of an approaching Messianic kingdom was dissipated, the idea of the perfect accomplishment of the will of God had to take the room of it, and in its own realisation to place the ideal of the true kingdom of God.

reaching their aim, presents fewer distractions, and, above all, supplies a more animating force of sympathy and mutual assurance, than the acting separately. Only the sense of differences greater than the sense of sympathy could defeat this tendency.

Cardinal Newman has told us what an impression was once made upon his mind by the sentence: *Securus judicat orbis terrarum.* I have shown how, for matters of philosophical judgment not yet settled but requiring development to clear them, the consent of the world, at a time when this clearing development cannot have happened, seems to carry little or no weight at all; indeed, as to judgment on these points, we might rather be inclined to lay down the very contrary of Dr. Newman's affirmation, and to say: *Securus delirat orbis terrarum.* But points of speculative theology being out of the question, and the practical ground and purpose of man's religion being broadly and plainly fixed, we should be quite disposed to concede to Dr. Newman, that *securus* colit *orbis terrarum;*—those pursue this purpose best who pursue it together. For unless prevented by extraneous causes, they manifestly tend, as the history of the Church's growth shows, to pursue it together.

Nonconformists are fond of talking of the unity which may co-exist with separation, and they say: 'There are four evangelists, yet one gospel; why should there not be many separate religious bodies, yet one Church?' But the Four Gospels arose out of no thought of divergency; they were not designed as corrections of one prior gospel, or of one another; they were concurring testimonies borne to the same fact. On the other hand, the several religious bodies of Christendom plainly grew out of an intention of divergency; clearly they were designed to correct the imperfections of one prior church and of each other; and to say of things sprung out of discord that they may make *one* because things sprung out of concord may make *one*, is like saying that because several agreements may make a peace, therefore several wars may make a peace too. No; without some strong motive to the contrary, men united by the pursuit of a clearly defined common aim of irresistible attractiveness naturally coalesce; and since they coalesce naturally, they are clearly right in coalescing and find their advantage in it.

All that Cardinal Newman has so excellently said about development applies here legitimately and fully. Existence justifies additions and stages in existence. The living edifice, planted on the foundation of Christ, could not but grow, if it lived at all. If it grew, it could not but make developments; and all developments not inconsistent with the aim of its original foundation, and not extending beyond the moral and practical sphere which was the sphere of its original foundation, are legitimated by the very fact of the Church having in the natural evolution of its life and growth made them. A boy does not wear the clothes or follow the ways of an infant, nor a man those of a boy; yet they are all engaged in the one same business of developing their growing life, and to the clothes to be worn and the ways to be followed for the purpose of doing this, nature will, in general, direct them safely. The several scattered congregations of the first age of Christianity coalesced into one community, just as the several scattered Christians had earlier still coalesced into congregations. Why?—because such was the natural course of things. It had nothing inconsistent with the fundamental duty of Christians to follow Christ; and it was approved by their growing and enlarging in it. They developed a church-discipline with a hierarchy of bishops and archbishops, which was not that of the first times; they developed church-usages, such as the practice of infant baptism, which were not those of the first times; they developed a church-ritual with ceremonies which were not those of the first times ;—they developed all these, just as they developed a church-architecture which was not that of the first times, because they were no longer in the first times, and required for their expanding growth what suited their own times. They coalesced with the State because they grew by doing so. They called the faith they possessed in common the *Catholic*, that is, the general or universal faith. They developed, also, as we have seen, dogma or a theological philosophy. Both dogma and discipline became a part of the Catholic faith, or profession of the general body of Christians.

Now to develop a discipline, or form of outward life for itself, the Church, as has been said, had necessarily, like every other living thing, the requisite qualifications ; to develop scientific dogma it had not. But even of the dogma which the Church developed it may be said, that, from the very nature of things, it was probably, as compared with the opposing dogma over which it prevailed, the more suited to the actual condition of the Church's life, and to the due progress of the divine work for which she existed. For instance, whatever may be scientifically the rights of the question about grace and free-will, it is evident that, for the Church of the fifth century, Pelagianism was the less inspiring and edifying doctrine, and the sense of *being in the divine hand* was the feeling which it was good for Christians to be filled with. Whatever may be scientifically the merits of the dispute between Arius and Athanasius, for the Church of their time whatever most exalted or seemed to exalt Jesus Christ was clearly the profitable doctrine, the doctrine most helpful to that moral life which was the true life of the Church.

People, however, there were in abundance who differed on points both of discipline and of dogma from the rule which obtained in the Church, and who separated from her on account of that difference. These were the heretics :

separatists, as the name implies, *for the sake of opinions.*
And the very name, therefore, implies that they were wrong
in separating, and that the body which held together was
right ; because the Church exists, not for the sake of opinions,
but for the sake of moral practice, and a united endeavour
after this is stronger than a broken one. Valentinians,
Marcionites, Montanists, Donatists, Manichæans, Novatians,
Eutychians, Apollinarians, Nestorians, Arians, Pelagians,—
if they separated on points of discipline they were wrong,
because for developing its own fit outward conditions of life
the body of a community has, as we have seen, a real
natural power, and individuals are bound to sacrifice their
fancies to it; if they separated on points of dogma they were
wrong also, because, while neither they nor the Church had
the means of determining such points adequately, the true
instinct lay in those who, instead of separating for such
points, conceded them as the Church settled them, and
found their bond of union, where it in truth really was,
not in notions about the co-eternity of the Son, but in
Christ's injunction, *Follow me!*

Does any one imagine that all the Church shared Augustine's speculative opinions about grace and predestination? that many members of it did not rather incline, as a matter of speculative opinion, to the notions of Pelagius? Does any one imagine that all who stood with the Church, and did not join themselves to the Arians, were speculatively Athanasians? It was not so ; but they had a true feeling for what purpose the Gospel and the Church were given them, and for what they were not given them ; they could see that 'impious and pious living,' according to that sentence of Epiphanius we have quoted from Hammond, 'divided the whole Christian world into erroneous and orthodox ;' and that it was not worth while to suffer themselves to be divided for anything else.

And though it will be said that separatists for opinions on points of discipline and dogma have often asserted, and sometimes believed, that piety and impiety were vitally concerned in these points; yet here again the true religious instinct is that which discerns,—what is seldom so very obscure,—whether they are in truth thus vitally concerned or not; and, if they are not, cannot be perverted into fancying them concerned and breaking unity for them. This, I say, is the true religious instinct, the instinct which most clearly seizes the essence and aim of the Christian Gospel and of the Christian Church. But fidelity to it leaves, also, the way least closed to the admission of true developments of speculative thought, when the time is come for them, and to the incorporation of these true developments with the ideas and practice of Christians.

Is there not, then, any separation which is right and reasonable? Yes, separation on plain points of morals. For these involve the very essence of the Christian Gospel, and the very ground on which the Christian Church is built. The sale of indulgences, if deliberately instituted and persisted in by the main body of the Church, afforded a valid reason for breaking unity; the doctrine of purgatory, or of the real presence, did not.

However, a cosmopolitan church-order, commenced when the political organisation of Christians was also cosmopolitan, —when, that is, the nations of Europe were politically one in the unity of the Roman Empire,—might well occasion difficulties as the nations solidified into independent states with a keen sense of their independent life; so that, the cosmopolitan type disappearing for civil affairs, and being replaced by the national type, the same disappearance and replacement tended to prevail in ecclesiastical affairs also. But this was a political difficulty, not a religious one, and it raised no insuperable bar to continued religious union. A

Church with Anglican liberties might very well, the English national spirit being what it is, have been in religious communion with Rome, and yet have been safely trusted to maintain and develop its national liberties to any extent required.

The moral corruptions of Rome, on the other hand, were a real ground for separation. On their account, and solely on their account, if they could not be got rid of, was separation not only lawful but necessary. It has always been the averment of the Church of England, that the change made in her at the Reformation was the very least change which was absolutely necessary. No doubt she used the opportunity of her breach with Rome to get rid of several doctrines which the human mind had outgrown; but it was the immoral practice of Rome that really moved her to separation. And she maintained that she merely got rid of Roman corruptions which were immoral and intolerable, and remained the old, historic, Catholic Church of England still.

The right to this title of *Catholic* is a favourite matter of contention between bodies of Christians. But let us use names in their customary and natural senses. To me it seems that unless one chooses to fight about words, and fancifully to put into the word *Catholic* some occult quality, one must allow that the changes made in the Church of England at the Reformation impaired its Catholicity. The word *Catholic* was meant to describe the common or general profession and worship of Christendom at the time when the word arose. Undoubtedly this general profession and worship had not a strict uniformity everywhere, but it had a clearly-marked common character; and this well-known type Bede, or Anselm, or Wiclif himself, would to this day easily recognise in a Roman Catholic religious service, but hardly in an Anglican; while, on the other hand, in a Roman Catholic religious service an ordinary Anglican finds

I

himself as much in a strange world and out of his usual course as in a Nonconformist meeting-house. Something precious was no doubt lost in losing this common profession and worship; but the loss was, as Protestants maintain, incurred for the sake of something yet more precious still,— the purity of that moral practice which was the very cause for which the common profession and worship existed. Now, it seems captious to incur voluntarily a loss for a great and worthy object, and at the same time, by a conjuring with words, to try and make it appear that we have not suffered the loss at all. So on the word *Catholic* we will not insist too jealously; but thus much, at any rate, must be allowed to the Church of England,—that she kept enough of the past to preserve, as far as this nation was concerned, her continuity, to be still the *historic Church of England*; and that she avoided the error, to which there was so much to draw her, and into which all the other reformed Churches fell, of making improved speculative doctrinal opinions the main ground of her separation.

A Nonconformist newspaper, it is true, reproaching the Church with what is, in our opinion, her greatest praise, namely, that on points of doctrinal theology she is 'a Church that does not know her own mind,' roundly asserts, as we have already mentioned, that 'no man in his senses can deny that the Church of England was meant to be a thoroughly Protestant and Evangelical, and it may be said Calvinistic Church.' But not only does the whole course of Church-history disprove such an assertion, and show that this is what the Puritans always wanted to make the Church, and what the Church would never be made, but we can disprove it, too, out of the mouths of the very Puritans themselves. At the Savoy Conference the Puritans urged that 'our first reformers did at that time (of the Reformation) so compose the Liturgy, as to win upon the Papists, and to draw them into their Church communion *by varying as little as they could from the Romish forms before in use* ;' and this they alleged as their great plea for purging the Liturgy. And the Bishops resisted, and upheld the proceeding of the reformers as the essential policy of the Church of England ; as indeed it was, and till this day has continued to be. No ; the Church of England did not give her energies to inventing a new church-order for herself and fighting for it ; to singling out two or three speculative dogmas as the essence of Christianity, and fighting for them. She set herself to carry forward, and as much as possible on the old lines, the old practical work and proper design of the Christian Church ; and this is what left her mind comparatively open, as we have seen, for the admission of philosophy and criticism, as they slowly developed themselves outside the Church and filtered into her ; an admission which confessedly proves just now to be of capital importance.

This openness of mind the Puritans have not shared with the Church, and how *should* they have shared it? They are founded on the negation of that idea of development which plays so important a part in the life of the Church ; on the assumption that there is a divinely appointed church-order fixed once for all in the Bible, and that they have adopted it ; that there is a doctrinal scheme of faith, justification, and imputed righteousness, which is the test of a standing or falling church and the essence of the gospel, and that they have extracted it. These are assumptions which, as they make union impossible, so also make growth impossible. The Church makes church-order a matter of ecclesiastical constitution, is founded on moral practice, and though she develops speculative dogma, does not allow that this or that dogma is the essence of Christianity.

'Congregational Nonconformists,' say the Independents,

'can never be incorporated into an organic union with Anglican Episcopacy, because there is not even the shadow of an outline of it in the New Testament, and it is our assertion and profound belief that Christ and the Apostles have given us all the laws that are necessary for the constitution and government of the Church.'[1] 'Whatever may come,' says the President of the Wesleyan Conference, 'we are determined to be simple, earnest preachers of *the gospel*. Whatever may come, we are determined to be true to *Scriptural Protestantism*. We would be friendly with all evangelical churches, but we will have no fellowship with the man of sin. We will give up life itself rather than be unfaithful to *the truth*. It is ours to cry everywhere : " Come, sinners, to *the gospel-feast!*"' And this *gospel*, this *Scriptural Protestantism*, this *truth*, is the doctrine of justification by 'pleading solely the blood of the covenant,' of which we have said so much. Methodists cannot unite with a church which does not found itself on this doctrine of justification, but which holds the doctrine of priestly absolution, of the real presence, and other doctrines of like stamp; Congregationalists cannot unite with a church which, besides not resting on the doctrine of justification, has a church-order not prescribed in the New Testament.

Now as Hooker truly says of those who 'desire to draw all things unto the determination of bare and naked Scripture,' as Cardinal Newman, too, has said, and as many others have said, the Bible does not exhibit, drawn out in black and white, the precise tenets and usages of any Christian society; some inference and criticism must be employed to get at them. 'For the most part, even such as are readiest to cite for one thing five hundred sentences of Scripture, what warrant have they that any one of them doth

[1] Address of the Rev. G. W. Conder at Liverpool, in the *Lancashire Congregational Calendar* for 1869-70.

mean the thing for which it is alleged?' Nay, 'it is not the word of God itself which doth, or possibly can, assure us that we do well to think it his word.' So says Hooker, and what he says is perfectly true. A process of reasoning and collection is necessary to get at the Scriptural church-discipline and the Scriptural Protestantism of the Puritans; in short, this discipline and this doctrine are developments. And the first is an unsound development, in a line where there was a power of making a true development, and where the Church made it; the second is an unsound development in a line where neither the Church nor Puritanism had the power of making true developments. But as it is the truth of its Scriptural Protestantism which in Puritanism's eyes especially proves the truth of its Scriptural church-order which has this Protestantism, and the falsehood of the Anglican church-order which has much less of it, to abate the confidence of the Puritans in their Scriptural Protestantism is the first step towards their union, so much to be desired, with the national Church.

We say, therefore, that the doctrine: 'It is agreed between God and the mediator Jesus Christ, the Son of God, surety for the redeemed, as parties-contractors, that the sins of the redeemed should be imputed to innocent Christ, and he both condemned and put to death for them upon this very condition, that whosoever heartily consents unto the covenant of reconciliation offered through Christ shall, by the imputation of his obedience unto them, be justified and holden righteous before God,'—we say that this doctrine is as much a human development from the text, 'Christ Jesus came into the world to save sinners,' as the doctrine of priestly absolution is a human development from the text, 'Whosesoever sins ye remit, they are remitted unto them,' or the doctrine of the real presence from the text, 'Take, eat, this is my body.' In our treatise on St. Paul we have shown at length how the received doctrine of justification is an unsound development. It may be said that the doctrine of priestly absolution and of the real presence are unsound developments also. True, in our opinion they are so ; they are, like the doctrine of justification, developments made under conditions which precluded the possibility of sound developments in this line. But the difference is here : the Church of England does not identify Christianity with these unsound developments ; she does not call either of them *Scriptural Protestantism*, or *truth*, or *the gospel* ; she does not insist that all who are in communion with her should hold them ; she does not repel from her communion those who hold doctrines at variance with them. She treats them as she does the received doctrine of justification, to which she does not tie herself up, but leaves people to hold it if they please. She thus provides room for growth and further change in these very doctrines themselves. But to the doctrine of justification Puritanism ties itself up, just as it tied itself up formerly to the doctrine of predestination ; it calls it *Scriptural Protestantism*, *truth*, *the gospel* ; it will have communion with none who do not hold it ; it repels communion with any who hold the doctrines of priestly absolution and the real presence, because these doctrines seem to interfere with it. Yet it is really itself no better than they. And how can growth possibly find place in this doctrine, while it is held in such a fashion ?

Every one who perceives and values the power contained in Christianity, must be struck to see how, at the present moment, the progress of this power seems to depend upon its being able to disengage itself from speculative accretions which encumber it. A considerable movement to this end is visible in the Church of England. But the larger the body in which this movement works, the greater is the power of the movement. If the Church of England were disestablished to-day it would be desirable to re-establish her to-morrow, if only because of the immense power for development which a national body possesses. It is because I know something of the Nonconformist ministers, and what eminent force and faculty many of them have for contributing to the work of development now before the Church, that I cannot bear to see the waste of power caused by their separatism and battling with the Establishment, which absorb their energies too much to suffer them to carry forward the work of development themselves, and cut them off from aiding those in the Church who carry it forward.

The political dissent of the Nonconformists, based on their condemnation of the Anglican church-order as unscriptural, is just one of those speculative accretions which we have spoken of as encumbering religion. Politics are a good thing, and religion is a good thing; but they make a fractious mixture. 'The Nonconformity of England, and the Nonconformity alone, has been the salvation of England from Papal tyranny and kingly misrule and despotism.'[1] This is the favourite boast, the familiar strain; but this is really politics, and not religion at all. But righteousness is religion; and the Nonconformists say: 'Who have done so much for righteousness as we?' For as much righteousness as will go with politics, no one; for the sterner virtues, for the virtues of the Jews of the Old Testament; but these are only half of righteousness and not the essentially Christian half. We have seen how St. Paul tore himself in two, rent his life in the middle and began it again, because he was so dissatisfied with a righteousness which was, after all, in its main features, Puritan. And surely it can hardly be denied that the more eminently and exactly *Christian* type of righteousness is the type exhibited by Church worthies like Herbert, Ken, and Wilson, rather than that exhibited

[1] The Rev. G. W. Conder, *ubi supra*.

by the worthies of Puritanism; the cause being that these last mixed politics with religion so much more than did the first.

Paul, too, be it remembered, condemned disunion in the society of Christians as much as he declined politics. This is decisive against the Puritan allegation that it does not matter whether the society of Christians is united or not, and that there are even great advantages in separatism. If Anglicans maintained that their church-order was written in Scripture and a matter of divine command, then, Congregationalists maintaining the same thing, to the controversy between them there could be no end. But now, Anglicans maintaining no such thing, but that their church-order is a matter of historic development and natural expediency, that it has *grown*,—which is evident enough,—and that the essence of Christianity is in no wise concerned with such matters, why should not the Nonconformists adopt this moderate view of the case, which constrains them to no admission of inferiority, but only to the renouncing an imagined divine superiority and to the recognition of an existing fact, and allow Church bishops as a development of Catholic antiquity, just as they have now allowed Church music and Church architecture, which are developments of the same? Then might there arise a mighty and undistracted power of joint life, which would transform, probably, the doctrines of priestly absolution and the real presence, would transform, equally, the so-called *Scriptural Protestantism* of imputed righteousness, but would do more for real righteousness and for Christianity than has ever been done yet.

Tillotson's proposals for comprehension, drawn up in 1689, cannot be too much studied at the present juncture. These proposals, with which his name and that of Stillingfleet, two of the most estimable names in the English Church, are specially associated, humiliate no one, refute no one; they take the basis of existing facts, and endeavour to build on it a solid union. They are worth quoting entire, and I conclude with them. Their details our present circumstances would modify; their spirit any sound plan of Church-reform must take as its rule.

'1. That the ceremonies enjoined or recommended in the Liturgy or Canons be left indifferent.

'2. That the Liturgy be carefully reviewed, and such alterations and changes be therein made as may supply the defects and remove as much as possible all ground of exception to any part of it, by leaving out the apocryphal lessons and correcting the translation of the psalms used in the public service where there is need of it, and in many other particulars.

'3. That instead of all former declarations and subscriptions to be made by ministers, it shall be sufficient for them that are admitted to the exercise of their ministry in the Church of England to subscribe one general declaration and promise to this purpose, viz. : *That we do submit to the doctrine, discipline, and worship of the Church of England as it shall be established by law, and promise to teach and practise accordingly.*

'4. That a new body of ecclesiastical Canons be made, particularly with a regard to a more effectual provision for the reformation of manners both in ministers and people.

'5. That there be an effectual regulation of ecclesiastical courts to remedy the great abuses and inconveniences which by degrees and length of time have crept into them; and particularly that the power of excommunication be taken out of the hands of lay officers and placed in the bishop, and not to be exercised for trivial matters, but upon great and weighty occasions.

'6. That for the future those who have been ordained

in any of the foreign churches be not required to be reordained here, to render them capable of preferment in the Church.

'7. That for the future none be capable of any ecclesiastical benefice or preferment in the Church of England that shall be ordained in England otherwise than by bishops; and that those who have been ordained only by presbyters shall not be compelled to renounce their former ordination. But because many have and do still doubt of the validity of such ordination, where episcopal ordination may be had, and is by law required, it shall be sufficient for such persons to receive ordination from a bishop in this or the like form: "If thou art not already ordained, I ordain thee," &c.; as in case a doubt be made of any one's baptism, it is appointed by the Liturgy that he be baptized in this form: "If thou art not baptized, I baptize thee."'

These are proposals 'to be made by the Church of England for the Union of *Protestants*.' Who cannot see that the power of joint life already spoken of would be far greater and stronger if it comprehended Roman Catholics too? And who cannot see, also, that a movement is possible which may at last bring about a general union of Christendom? But this will not be in our day, nor is it business which the England of this generation is set to do. What may be done in England in our day, what our generation has the call and the means, if only it has the resolution, to bring about, is the union of Protestants. But this union will never be on the basis of the actual *Scriptural Protestantism* of our Puritans; and because, so long as they take this for the gospel or good news of Christ, they cannot possibly unite on any other basis, the first step towards union is showing them that this is not the gospel. If I have succeeded in doing even so much towards union as to convince one of them of this, I have not written in vain.

MODERN DISSENT.

THE foregoing essay was meant to clear away offence or misunderstanding which had arisen out of the treatise on St. Paul and Protestantism. There still remain one or two points on which a word of explanation may be useful, and to them the present essay is addressed.

The general objection, that the scheme of doctrine criticised by me is common to both Puritanism and the Church of England, and does not characterise the one more essentially than the other, has been removed, I hope, by the preceding essay. But it is said that there is, at any rate, a large party in the Church of England,—the so-called *Evangelical* party,—which holds just the scheme of doctrine I have called Puritan; that this large party, at least, if not the whole Church of England, is as much a stronghold of the distinctive Puritan tenets as the Nonconformists are; and that to tax the Nonconformists with these tenets, and to say nothing about the Evangelical clergy holding them too, is injurious and unfair.

The Evangelical party in the Church of England we must always, certainly, have a disposition to treat with forbearance, inasmuch as this party has so strongly loved what is indeed the most loveable of things,—religion. The Evangelicals have also avoided that unblessed mixture of politics and religion by which both politics and religion are spoilt. This, however, would not alone have prevented our making them jointly answerable with the Puritans for that body of opinions, which calls itself Scriptural Protestantism, but which is, in truth, a perversion of St. Paul's Epistle to the Romans. But there is this difference between the Evangelical party in the Church of England and the Puritans outside her : the Evangelicals have not added to the first error of holding this unsound body of opinions the second error of separating for them. They have thus, as we have already noticed, escaped the mixing of politics and religion, which arises directly and naturally out of this separating for opinions. But they have also done that which we most blame Nonconformity for not doing ;—they have left themselves in the way of development. Practically they have admitted that the Christian Church is built, not on the foundation of Lutheran and Calvinist dogmas, but on the injunction of Jesus, Follow me. Bishop Ryle or Dean Close may have as erroneous notions as to what *truth and the Gospel* really is, as Mr. Spurgeon or the President of the Wesleyan Conference ; but they do not tie themselves tighter still to these erroneous notions, nor do their best to cut themselves off from outgrowing them, by resolving *to have no fellowship with the man of sin* who holds different notions. On the contrary, they are worshippers in the same Church, professors of the same faith, ministers of the same confraternity, as men who hold that their *Scriptural Protestantism* is all wrong, and who hold other notions of their own quite at variance with it. And thus they do homage to an ideal of Christianity which is larger, higher, and better than either their notions or those of their opponents, and in respect of which both their notions and those of their opponents are inadequate ; and this admission of the relative inadequacy of their notions is itself a stage towards the future admission of their positive inadequacy.

In fact, the popular Protestant theology, which we have criticised as such a grave perversion of the teaching of St.

Paul, has not now in the so-called Evangelical party of the Church of England its chief centre and stronghold. This party, which, following in the wake of Wesley and others, so felt in a day of general insensibility the power and comfort of the Christian religion, and which did so much to make others feel them, but which also adopted and promulgated a scientific account so inadequate and so misleading of the religion which attracted it,—this great party has done its work, and is now undergoing that law of transformation and development which obtains in a national Church. The power is passing from it to others, who will make good some of the aspects of religion which the Evangelicals neglected, and who will then, in their turn, from the same cause of the scientific inadequacy of their conception of Christianity, change and pass away. The Evangelical clergy no longer recruits itself with success, no longer lays hold on such promising subjects as formerly. It is losing the future and feels that it is losing it. Its signs of a vigorous life, its gaiety and audacity, are confined to its older members, too powerful to lose their own vigour, but without successors to whom to transmit it. It was impossible not to admire the genuine and rich though somewhat brutal humour of the Dean of Ripon's famous similitude of the two lepers.[1] But from which of the younger members of the Evangelical clergy do such strokes now come? The best of their own younger generation, the soldiers of their own training, are slipping away from them; and he who

---

[1] In a letter to the *Times* respecting Dr. Pusey and Dr. Temple, during the discussion caused by Dr. Temple's appointment to the see of Exeter. Dr. Temple was the total leper, so evidently a leper that all men would instinctively avoid him, and he ceased to be dangerous; Dr. Pusey was the partial leper, less deeply tainted, but on that very account more dangerous, because less likely to terrify people from coming near him. A piece of polemical humour, racy, indeed, but hardly urbane, and still less Christian!

looks for the source whence popular Puritan theology now derives power and perpetuation, will not fix his eyes on the Evangelical clergy of the Church of England.

Another point where a word of explanation seems desirable is the objection taken on a kind of personal ground to the criticism of St. Paul's doctrine which I have attempted. 'What!' it is said, 'if this view of St. Paul's meaning, so unlike the received view, were the true one, do you suppose it would have been left for you to discover it? Are you wiser than the hundreds of learned people who for generation after generation have been occupying themselves with St. Paul and little else? Has it been left for you to bring in a new religion and found a new church?' Now on this line of expostulation, which, so far as it draws from unworthiness of ours its argument, appears to have, no doubt, great force, there are three remarks to be offered. In the first place, even if the version of St. Paul which we propound were both new and true, yet we do not, on that account, make of it a new religion or set up a new church for its sake. That would be *separating for opinions*, heresy, which is just what we reproach the Nonconformists with. In the seventh century, there arose near the Euphrates a sect called Paulicians, who professed to form themselves on the pure doctrine of St. Paul, which other Christians, they said, had misunderstood and corrupted. And we, I suppose, having discovered how popular Protestantism perverts St. Paul, are expected to try and make a new sect of Paulicians on the strength of this discovery; such being just the course which our Puritan friends would themselves eagerly take in like case. But the Christian Church is founded, not on a correct speculative knowledge of the ideas of Paul, but on much surer ground: on Christ's command, *Follow me*; and, holding this to be so, we might change the current strain of doctrinal theology from one end to the other, without, on that account, setting up any new church or bringing in any new religion.

In the second place, the version we propound of St. Paul's line of thought is not new, is not of our discovering. It belongs to the 'Zeit-Geist,' or *time-spirit*, it is in the air, and many have long been anticipating it, preparing it, setting forth this and that part of it, till there is not a part, probably, of all we have said, which has not already been said by others before us, and said more learnedly and fully than we can say it. All we have done is to take it as a whole, and give a plain, popular, connected, exposition of it.

Thirdly, and in the last place, we by no means put forth our version of St. Paul's line of thought as true, in the same fashion as Puritanism puts forth its *Scriptural Protestantism*, or *gospel*, as true. Their truth the Puritans exhibit as a sort of cast-iron product, rigid, definite, and complete, which they have got once for all, and which can no longer have anything added to it or anything withdrawn from it. But of our rendering of St. Paul's thought we conceive rather as of a product of nature, which has grown to be what it is and which will grow more; which will not stand just as we now exhibit it, but which will gain some aspects which we now fail to show in it, and will drop some which we now give to it; which will be developed, in short, farther, just in like manner as it has reached its present stage by development.

Thus we present our conceptions, neither as something quite new nor as something quite true; nor yet as any ground, even supposing they were quite new and true, for a separate church or religion. But so far they are, we think, new and true, and a fruit of sound development, a genuine product of the 'Zeit-Geist,' that their mere contact seems to make the old Puritan conceptions look unlikely and indefensible, and begin a sort of remodelling and refacing of themselves. Let us just see how far this change has practically gone.

The formal and scholastic version of its theology, Calvinist or Arminian, as given by its seventeenth-century fathers, and enshrined in the trust-deeds of so many of its chapels,—of this, at any rate, modern Puritanism is beginning to feel shy. Take the Calvinist doctrine of election. 'By God's decree a certain number of angels and men are predestinated, out of God's mere free grace and love, without any foresight of faith or good works in them, to everlasting life; and others foreordained, according to the unsearchable counsel of his will, whereby he extends or withholds mercy as he pleases, to everlasting death.' In that scientific form, at least, the doctrine of election begins to look dubious to the Calvinistic Puritan, and he puts it a good deal out of sight. Take the Arminian doctrine of justification. 'We could not expect any relief from heaven out of that misery under which we lie, were not God's displeasure against us first pacified and our sins remitted. This is the signal and transcendent benefit of our free justification through the blood of Christ, that God's offence justly conceived against us for our sins (which would have been an eternal bar and restraint to the efflux of his grace upon us) being removed, the divine grace and bounty may freely flow forth upon us.' In that scientific form, the doctrine of justification begins to look less satisfactory to the Arminian Puritan, and he tends to put it out of sight.

The same may be said of the doctrine of election in its plain popular form of statement also. 'I hold,' says Whitfield, in the forcible style which so took his hearers' fancy,—'I hold that a certain number are elected from eternity, and these must and shall be saved, and the rest of mankind must and shall be damned.' A Calvinistic Puritan now-a-days must be either a fervid Welsh Dissenter, or a strenuous

Particular Baptist in some remote place in the country, not to be a little staggered at this sort of expression. As to the doctrine of justification in its current, popular form of statement, the case is somewhat different. 'My own works,' says Wesley, 'my own sufferings, my own righteousness, are so far from reconciling me to an offended God, that the most specious of them need an atonement themselves. I have no hope but that of being justified freely through the redemption that is in Jesus. The faith I want is a sure trust and confidence in God, that through the merits of Christ my sins are forgiven and I reconciled to the favour of God. Believe and thou shalt be saved! He that believeth is passed from death to life. Look for sanctification just as you are, as a poor sinner that has nothing to pay, nothing to plead but *Christ died.*' Deliverances of this sort, which in Wesley are frequent and in Wesley's followers are unceasing, still, no doubt, pass current everywhere with Puritanism, are expected as of course, and find favour; they are just what Puritans commonly mean by *Scriptural Protestantism, the truth, the gospel-feast.* Nevertheless they no longer quite satisfy; the better minds among Puritans try instinctively to give some fresh turn or development to them; they are no longer, to minds of this order, an unquestionable word and a sure stay; and from this point to their final transformation the course is certain. The predestinarian and solifidian dogmas, for the very sake of which our Puritan churches came into existence, begin to feel the irresistible breath of the 'Zeit-Geist;' some of them melt quicker, others slower, but all of them are doomed. Under the eyes of this generation Puritan Dissent has to execute an entire change of front, and to present us with a new reason for its existing. What will that new reason be?

There needs no conjuror to tell us. It will be the Rev. Mr. Conder's reason, which we have quoted in our pre-

K

ceding essay. It will be Scriptural Protestantism in *church-order*, rather than Scriptural Protestantism in *church-doctrine*. 'Congregational Nonconformists can never be incorporated into an organic union with Anglican Episcopacy, because there is not even the shadow of an outline of it in the New Testament, and it is our assertion and profound belief that Christ and the Apostles have given us all the laws that are necessary for the constitution and government of the Church.' This makes church-government not a secondary matter of form, growth, and expediency, but a matter of the essence of Christianity and ordained in Scripture. Expressly set forth in Scripture it is not; so it has to be gathered from Scripture by collection, and everyone gathers it in his own way. Unity is of no great importance; but that every man should live in a church-order which he judges to be scriptural, is of the greatest importance. This brings us to Mr. Miall's standard-maxim: *The Dissidence of Dissent, and the Protestantism of the Protestant religion !* The more freely the sects develop themselves, the better. The Church of England herself is but *the dominant sect*; her pretensions to bring back the Dissenters within her pale are offensive and ridiculous. What we ought to aim at is perfect equality, and that the other sects should balance her.

On the old, old subject of the want of historic and philosophic sense shown by those who would make church-government a matter of scriptural regulation, I say nothing at present. A Wesleyan minister, the Rev. Mr. Willey, said to an applauding audience: 'He did not find anything in either the old or New Testament to the effect that Christian ministers should become State-servants, like soldiers or excisemen.' He might as well have added that he did not find there anything to the effect that they should wear braces! But on this point I am not here going to enlarge

What I am now concerned with is the relation of this new ground of existence, which more and more the Puritan Churches take and will take as they lose their old ground, to the Christian religion. In the speech which Mr. Winterbotham[1] made on the Education Bill, a speech which I had the advantage of hearing, there were uncommon facilities supplied for judging of this relation; indeed that able speech presented a striking picture of it.

And what a picture it was, good heavens! The Puritans say they love righteousness, and they are offended with me for rejoining that the righteousness of which they boast is the righteousness of the earlier Jews of the Old Testament, which consisted mainly in smiting the Lord's enemies and their own under the fifth rib. And we say that the newer and specially Christian sort of righteousness is something different from this; that the Puritans are, and always have been, deficient in the specially Christian sort of righteousness; that men like St. Francis of Sales, in the Roman Catholic Church, and Bishop Wilson, in the Church of England, show far more of it than any Puritans; and that St. Paul's signal and eternally fruitful growth in righteousness dates just from his breach with the Puritans of his day. Let us revert to Paul's list of fruits of the spirit, on which we have so often insisted in the pages which precede: *love, joy, peace, patience, kindness, goodness, faith, mildness, self-control.*[2] We keep to this particular list for the sake of greater distinctness; but St. Paul has perpetually lists of the kind, all pointing the same way, and all showing what he meant by Christian righteousness, what he found specially in

---

[1] Mr. Winterbotham has since died. Nothing in my remarks on his speech need prevent me from expressing here my high esteem for his character, accomplishments, oratorical faculty and general promise, and my sincere regret for his loss.

[2] *Gal.*, v, 22, 23.

Christ. They may all be concluded in two qualities, the qualities which Jesus Christ told his disciples to learn of him, the qualities in the name of which, as specially Christ's qualities, Paul adjured his converts. 'Learn of me,' said Jesus, *'that I am mild and lowly in heart.'* 'I beseech you,' said Paul, *'by the mildness and gentleness of Christ.'* [1] The word which our Bibles translate by 'gentleness,' means more properly 'reasonableness with sweetness,' 'sweet reasonableness.' 'I beseech you by *the mildness and sweet reasonableness of Christ.'* This mildness and sweet reasonableness it was, which, stamped with the individual charm they had in Jesus Christ, came to the world as something new, won its heart and conquered it. Every one had been asserting his ordinary self and was miserable; to forbear to assert one's ordinary self, to place one's happiness in mildness and sweet reasonableness, was a revelation. As men followed this novel route to happiness, a living spring opened beside their way, the spring of charity; and out of this spring arose those two heavenly visitants, Charis and Irene, *grace* and *peace*, which enraptured the poor wayfarer, and filled him with a joy which brought all the world after him. And still whenever these visitants appear, as appear for a witness to the vitality of Christianity they daily do, it is from the same spring that they arise; and this spring is opened solely by the mildness and sweet reasonableness which forbears to assert our ordinary self, nay, which even takes pleasure in effacing it.

And now let us turn to Mr. Winterbotham and the Protestant Dissenters. He interprets their very inner mind, he says; that which he declares in their name, they are all feeling, and would declare for themselves if they could. '*There was a spirit of watchful jealousy on the part of the Dissenters, which made them prone to take offence; therefore statesmen*

---

[1] διὰ τῆς πραΰτητος καὶ ἐπιεικείας τοῦ Χριστοῦ. II *Cor.*, x, I.

should not introduce the Established Church into all the institutions of the country.' That is positively the whole speech ! 'Strife, jealousy, wrath, contentions, backbitings,'[1] —we know the catalogue. And the Dissenters are, by their own confession, so full of these, and the very existence of an organisation of Dissent so makes them a necessity, that the state is required to frame its legislation in consideration of them ! Was there ever such a confession made? Here are people existing for the sake of a religion of which the essence is mildness and sweet reasonableness, and the forbearing to assert our ordinary self ; and they declare themselves so full of the very temper and habits against which that religion is specially levelled, that they require to have even the occasion of forbearing to assert their ordinary self removed out of their way, because they are quite sure they will never be equal to it !

Never was there a more instructive comment on the blessings of separation, which we are so often invited by separatists to admire. Why does not Dissent forbear to assert its ordinary self, and help to win the world to the mildness and sweet reasonableness of Christ, without this vain contest about machinery? Why does not the Church? is the Dissenter's answer. What an answer for a Christian ! We are to defer giving up our ordinary self until our neighbour shall have given up his ; that is, we are never to give it up at all. But I will answer the question on more mundane grounds. Why are we to be more blamed than the Church for the strife arising out of our rival existences ? asks the Dissenter. Because the Church cannot help existing, and you can ! Therefore *contra ecclesiam nemo pacificus*, as Baxter himself said in his better moments. Because the Church is there ; because strife, jealousy, and self-assertion are sure to come with breaking

[1] II *Cor.*, xii, 20.

off from her; and because strife, jealousy, and self-assertion are the very miseries against which Christianity is firstly levelled;—therefore we say that a Christian is inexcusable in breaking with the Church, except for a departure from that primal ground of her foundation: *Let every one that invokes the name of Christ depart from iniquity.*[1]

The clergyman,—poor soul!—cannot help being the parson of the parish. He is there like the magistrate; he is a national officer with an appointed function. If one or two voluntary performers, dissatisfied with the magisterial system, were to set themselves up in each parish of the country, called themselves magistrates, drew a certain number of people to their own way of thinking, tried differences and gave sentences among their people in the best fashion they could, why, probably the established magistrate would not much like it, the leading people in the parish would not much like it, and the new-comers would have mortifications and social estrangements to endure. Probably the established magistrate would call them interlopers; probably he would count them amongst his difficulties. On the side of the new-comers 'a spirit of watchful jealousy,' as Mr. Winterbotham says, would thus be created. The public interest would suffer from the ill blood and confusion prevailing. The established magistrate might naturally say that the new-comers brought the strife and disturbance with them. But who would not smile at these lambs answering: 'Away with that wolf the established magistrate, and all ground for jealousy and quarrel between us will disappear!'

And it is a grievance that the clergyman talks of Dissent as one of the spiritual hindrances in his parish and desires to get rid of it! Why, by Mr. Winterbotham's own showing, the Dissenters live 'in a spirit of watchful jealousy,' and this

[1] II *Tim.*, ii, 19.

temper is as much a spiritual hindrance,—nay, in the view of Christianity it is even a more direct spiritual hindrance,—than drunkenness or loose living. Christianity is, first and above all, a temper, a disposition; and a disposition just the opposite to 'a spirit of watchful jealousy.' Once admit a spirit of watchful jealousy, and Christianity has lost its virtue; it is impotent. All the other vices it was meant to keep out may rush in. Where there is jealousy and strife among you, asks St. Paul, *are ye not carnal?*[1] are ye not still in bondage to your mere lower selves? But from this bondage Christianity was meant to free us; therefore, says he, get rid of what causes divisions, and strife, and 'a spirit of watchful jealousy.' 'I exhort you by the name of our Lord Jesus Christ that ye all speak the same thing, and that there be not divisions among you, but that ye all be perfectly joined in the same mind and the same judgment.'[2]

Well, but why, says the Dissenting minister, is the clergyman to impress St. Paul's words upon me rather than I upon the clergyman? Because the clergyman, I repeat, is the one minister of Christ in the parish who did not invent himself, who cannot help existing. He is not asserting his ordinary self by being there; he is placed there on public duty. He is charged with teaching the lesson of Christianity, and the head and front of this lesson is to get rid of 'a spirit of watchful jealousy,' which, according to the Dissenter's own showing, is the very spirit which accompanies Dissent. How he is to get rid of it, how he is to win souls to the mildness and sweet reasonableness of Christ, it is for his own conscience to tell him. Probably he will best do it by never speaking against Dissent at all, by treating Dissenters with perfect cordiality and as if there was not a point of dispute between them. But that, so long as he exists, it is his duty to get rid of Dissent, to win souls to the unity which is its opposite, is clear. It is

[1] 1 *Cor.*, iii, 3.   [2] 1 *Cor.*, i, 10.

not the Bishop of Winchester[1] who classes Dissent, full of
'a spirit of watchful jealousy,' along with spiritual hindrances
like beer-shops,—a pollution of the spirit along with pollu-
tions of the flesh;[2] it is St. Paul. It is not the clergyman
who is chargeable with wishing to 'stamp out' this spirit;
it is the Christian religion.

But what is to prevent the Dissenting minister from
being joined with the clergyman in the same public function,
and being his partner instead of his rival? The requirement
of episcopal ordination, we are told, prevents it.[3] But if I
leave the service of a private company and enter the
public service, I must receive admission at the hands of
the public officer designated to give it me. Sentiment and
the historic sense, to say nothing of the religious feeling,
will certainly put more into ordination than this, though not
precisely what the Bishop of Winchester, perhaps, puts;
this which we have laid down, however, is really all which
the law of the land puts there. A bishop is a public officer.
Why should I trouble myself about the name his office
bears? The name of his office cannot affect the service or
my labour in it. Ah, but, says Mr. Winterbotham, he holds
opinions which I do not share about the sort of character he
confers upon me! What can that matter, unless he compels
you, too, to profess the same opinions, or refuses you admission if you do not? But I should be joined in the

---

[1] The late Bishop Wilberforce. [2] 1 *Cor.*, vii, 1.

[3] It has been inferred from what is here said that I propose to
make re-ordination a condition of admitting Dissenting ministers to the
ministry of the Church of England. Elsewhere I have said how
undesirable it seems to impose this condition; and to what respectful
treatment and fair and equal terms, in case of reunion, Protestant
Nonconformity is, in my opinion, entitled. See the Preface to *Culture
and Anarchy.* What is said in the text is directed simply against the
objection to episcopal ordination as something wrong in itself and a
ground for schism.

ministry with men who hold opinions which I do not share! What does that matter either, unless they compel you also to hold these opinions, as the price of your being allowed to work for Christ's kingdom? To recur to our old parallel. It is as if a man who desired the office of a public magistrate, and who was fitted for it, were to hold off because he had to receive institution from a Lord-Lieutenant, and he did not like the title of Lord-Lieutenant; or because the Lord-Lieutenant who was to institute him had a fancy about some occult quality which he conferred on him at institution; or because he would find himself, when he was instituted, one of a body of magistrates of whom many had notions which he thought irrational. The office itself, and his own power to fill it usefully, is all which really matters to him.

The Bishop of Winchester believes in apostolical succession;—therefore there must be Dissenters. Mr. Liddon asserts the real presence;—therefore there must be Dissenters. Mr. Mackonochie is a ritualist;—therefore there must be Dissenters. But the Bishop of Winchester cannot, and does not, exclude from the ministry of the Church of England those who do not believe in apostolical succession; and surely not even that acute and accomplished personage is such a magician, that he can make a Puritan believe in apostolical succession merely by believing in it himself. In the same way, eloquent as is Mr. Liddon and devoted as is Mr. Mackonochie, their gifts cannot yield them the art of so swaying a brother clergyman's spirit as to make him admit the real presence against his conviction, or practise ritualism against his will; and official, material control over him, or power of stipulating what he shall admit or practise, they have absolutely none.

But can anything more tend to make the Church what the Puritans reproach it with being,—a mere lump of sacerdotalism and ritualism,—than if the Puritans, who are free to come into it with their disregard of sacerdotalism and ritualism, and so to leaven it, refuse to come in, and leave it wholly to the sacerdotalists and ritualists? What can be harder upon the laity of the national Church, what so inconsiderate of the national good and advantage, as to leave us at the mercy of one single element in the Church, and deny us just the elements fit to mix with this element and to improve it?

The current doctrines of apostolical succession and the real presence seem to me unsound and unedifying. To be sure, so does the current doctrine of imputed righteousness. For me, sacerdotalism and solifidianism stand both on the same footing; they are, both of them, erroneous human developments. But as in the ideas and practice of sacerdotalists or ritualists there is much which seems to me of value, and of great use to the Church, so, too, in the ideas and practice of Nonconformists there is very much to value. To take points only that are beyond controversy: they have cultivated the gift of preaching much more than the clergy, and their union with the Church would renovate and immensely amend Church preaching. They would certainly bring with them, if they came back into the Church, some use of what they call *free prayer*; to which, if at present they give far too much place, it is yet to be regretted that the Church gives no place at all. Lastly, if the body of British Protestant Dissenters is in the main, as it undoubtedly is, the Church of the middle-class Philistines, nevertheless there could come nothing but health and strength from blending this body with the Establishment, of which the very weakness and danger is that it tends, as we have formerly said, to be an appendage to the upper-class Barbarians.

So long as the Puritans thought that the essence of Christianity was their doctrine of predestination or of justification, it was natural that they should stand out, at any cost, for this essence. That is why, when the 'Zeit-Geist' and the general movement of men's religious ideas is beginning to reveal that the Puritan gospel is not the essence of Christianity, we have been desirous to spread this revelation to the best of our power, and by all the aids of plain popular exposition to help it forward. Because, when once it is clear that the essence of Christianity is not Puritan solifidianism, it can hardly long be maintained that the essence of Christianity is Puritan church-order. When once the way is made clear, by removing the solifidian heresy, to look and see what the essence of Christianity really is, it cannot but soon force itself upon our minds that the essence of Christianity is something not very far, at any rate, from this: *Grace and peace by the annulment of our ordinary self through the mildness and sweet reasonableness of Jesus Christ.* This is the more particular description of that general ground, already laid down, of the Christian Church's existence: Jesus Christ's injunction, *Follow me.* If this general ground, particularised in the way above given, is not 'the sincere milk' of the evangelical word, it is, at all events, something very like it. And matters of machinery and outward form, like church-order, have not only nothing essentially to do with the sincere milk of Christianity, but are the very matters about which this sincere milk should make us easy and yielding.

If there were no national and historic form of church-order in possession of the field, a genuine Christian would regret having to spend time and thought in shaping one, in having so to encumber himself with serving, to busy himself so much about a frame for his religious life as well as about the contents of the frame. After all, a man has only a certain sum of force to spend; and if he takes a quantity of it for outward things, he has so much the less left for inward things.

It is hardly to be believed, how much larger a space the mere affairs of his denomination fill in the time and thoughts of a Dissenter, than in the time and thoughts of a Churchman. Now all machinery-work of this kind is, to a man filled with a real love of the essence of Christianity, something of a hindrance to him in what he most wants to be at, something of a concession to his ordinary self. When an established and historic form exists, such a man should be, therefore, disposed to use it and comply with it. But,—as if it were not satisfied with proving its unprofitableness by corroding us with jealousy and so robbing us of the mildness and sweet reasonableness of Christ, which is the Christian's mainstay,—political Dissent, Dissent for the sake of church-polity and church-management, proves it, too, by stimulating our ordinary self through over-care for what flatters this. In fact, what is it that the everyday, middle-class Philistine,—not the rare flower of the Dissenters but the common staple,—finds so attractive in Dissent? Is it not, as to discipline, that his self-importance is fomented by the fuss, bustle, and partisanship of a private sect, instead of being lost in the greatness of a public body? As to worship, is it not that his taste is pleased by usages and words that come down to *him*, instead of drawing him up to *them* ; by services which reflect, instead of the culture of great men of religious genius, the crude culture of himself and his fellows? And as to doctrine, is it not that his mind is pleased at hearing no opinion but its own, by having all disputed points taken for granted in its own favour, by being urged to no return upon itself, no development? And what is all this but the very feeding and stimulating of our ordinary self, instead of the annulling of it? No doubt it is natural; to indulge our ordinary self is the most natural thing in the world. But Christianity is not natural; and if the flower of Christianity be the grace and peace which comes of annulling our ordinary self, then to this flower it is fatal.

So that if, in order to gratify in the Dissenters one or the two faults against which Christianity is chiefly aimed, a jealous, contentious spirit, we were to sweep away our national and historic form of religion, and were all to tinker at our own forms, we should then just be flattering the other chief fault which Christianity came to cure, and serving our ordinary self instead of annulling it. What a happy furtherance to religion!

For my part, so far as the best of the Nonconformist ministers are concerned, of whom I know something, I disbelieve Mr. Winterbotham's hideous confession. I imagine they are very little pleased with him for making it. I do not believe that they, at any rate, live in the ulcerated condition he describes, fretting with watchful jealousy. I believe they have other things to think of. But why? Because they are men of genius and character, who react against the harmful influences of the position in which they find themselves placed, and surmount its obvious dangers. But their genius and character might serve them still better if they were placed in a less trying position. And the rank and file of their ministers and people do yield to the influences of their position. Of these Mr. Winterbotham's picture is perfectly true. They are more and more jealous for their separate organisation, pleased with the bustle and self-importance which its magnitude brings them, irritably alive to whatever reduces or effaces it; bent, in short, on affirming their ordinary selves. However much the chiefs may feel the truth of modern ideas, may grow moderate, may perceive the effects of religious separatism upon worship and doctrine, they probably will avail little or nothing; the head runs risk of being overpowered and out-clamoured by the tail. The Wesleyans, who used always to refuse to call themselves Dissenters, whose best men still shrink from the name, the Wesleyans, a wing of the Church, founded for godliness, the Wesleyans more and more, with their very growth as a separate denomination, feel the secular ambition of being great as a denomination, of being effaced by nobody, of giving contentment to this self-importance, of indulging this ordinary self; and I should not wonder if within twenty years they were keen political Dissenters. A triumph of Puritanism is abundantly possible; we have never denied it. What we, whose greatest care is neither for the Church nor for Puritanism, but for human perfection, what we labour to show is, that the triumph of Puritanism will be the triumph of our ordinary self, not the triumph of Christianity; and that the type of Hebraism it will establish is one in which neither general human perfection, nor yet Hebraism itself, can truly find their account.

Elsewhere we have drawn out a distinction between Hebraism and Hellenism,[1]—between the tendency and powers that carry us towards doing, and the tendency and powers that carry us towards perceiving and knowing. Hebraism, we said, has long been overwhelmingly preponderant with us. The sacred book which we call the Word of God, and which many of us study far more than any other book, serves Hebraism. Moses Hebraises, David Hebraises, Isaiah Hebraises, Paul Hebraises, John Hebraises. Jesus Christ himself is, as St. Paul truly styles him, 'a minister *of the circumcision* to the truth of God.'[2] That is, it is by our powers of moral action, and through the perfecting of these, that Christ leads us 'to be partakers of the divine nature.'[3] By far our chief machinery for spiritual purposes has the like aim and character. Throughout Europe this is so. But, to speak of ourselves only,

---

[1] See *Culture and Anarchy*, chap. iv.
[2] *Rom.*, xv, 8.   [3] II Peter, i, 4.

the Archbishop of Canterbury is an agent of Hebraism, the Archbishop of York is an agent of Hebraism, Cardinal Manning is an agent of Hebraism, the President of the Wesleyan Conference is an agent of Hebraism, all the body of the Church clergy and Dissenting ministers are agents of Hebraism. Now, we have seen how we are beginning visibly to suffer harm from attending in this one-sided way to Hebraism, and how we are called to develop ourselves more in our totality, on our perceptive and intelligential side as well as on our moral side. If it is said that this is a very hard matter, and that man cannot well do more than one thing at a time, the answer is that here is the very sign and condition of each new stage of spiritual progress,—*increase of task*. The more we grow, the greater is the task which is set us. This is the law of man's nature and of his spirit's history. The powers we have developed at our old task enable us to attempt a new one; and this, again, brings with it a new increase of powers.

Hebraism strikes too exclusively upon one string in us; Hellenism does not address itself with serious energy enough to morals and righteousness. For our totality, for our general perfection, we need to unite the two; now the two are easily at variance. In their lower forms they are irreconcileably at variance; only when each of them is at its best, is their harmony possible. Hebraism at its best is beauty and charm; Hellenism at its best is also beauty and charm. As such they can unite; as anything short of this, each of them, they are at discord, and their separation must continue. The flower of Hellenism is a kind of amiable grace and artless winning good-nature, born out of the perfection of lucidity, simplicity, and natural truth; the flower of Christianity is grace and peace by the annulment of our ordinary self through the mildness and sweet reasonableness of Christ. Both are eminently *humane*, and for complete human perfection both are required; the second being the perfection of that side in us which is moral and acts, the first, of that side in us which is intelligential and perceives and knows.

But lower forms of Hebraism and Hellenism tend always to make their appearance, and to strive to establish themselves. On one of these forms of Hebraism we have here been commenting;—a form which had its first origin, no doubt, in that body of impulses whereby we Hebraise, but which lands us at last, not in the mildness and sweet reasonableness of Christ, but in 'a spirit of watchful jealousy.' We have to thank Mr. Winterbotham for fixing our attention on it; but we prefer to name it from an eminent and able man who is well known as the earnest apostle of 'the Dissidence of Dissent and the Protestantism of the Protestant religion,' and to call it *Mialism*. Mialism is a sub-form of Hebraism, and itself a somewhat spurious and degenerated form; but this sub-form always tends to degenerate into forms lower yet, and yet more unworthy of the ideal flower of Hebraism. In one of these its further stages we have formerly traced it, and we need not enlarge on them here.[1]

Hellenism, in the same way, has its more or less spurious and degenerated sub-forms, products which may be at once known as degenerations by their deflexion from what we have marked as the flower of Hellenism,—'a kind of humane grace and artless winning good-nature, born out of the perfection of lucidity, simplicity, and natural truth.' And from whom can we more properly derive a general name for these degenerations, than from that distinguished man, who, by his intelligence and accomplishments, was in some respects so admirable and so truly Hellenic, but whom his dislike for 'the dominant sect,' as he calls the Church of England,—the Church of England, in many aspects so

[1] See *Culture and Anarchy*, chap. ii.

beautiful, calming, and attaching,—seems to transport with an almost feminine vehemence of irritation? What can we so fitly name the somewhat degenerated and inadequate form of Hellenism as *Millism*? This is the Hellenic or Hellenistic counterpart of Mialism; and like Mialism it has its further degenerations, in which it is still less commendable than in its first form. For instance, what in Mr. Mill is but a yielding to a spirit of irritable injustice, goes on and worsens in some of his disciples, till it becomes a sort of mere blatancy and truculent hardness in certain of them, in whom there appears scarcely anything that is truly sound or Hellenic at all.

Mankind, however, must needs draw, however slowly, towards its perfection; and our only real perfection is our totality. Mialism and Millism we may see playing into one another's hands, and apparently acting together; but, so long as these lower forms of Hellenism and Hebraism prevail, the real union between Hellenism and Hebraism can never be accomplished, and our totality is still as far off as ever. Unhappy and unquiet alternations of ascendency between Hebraism and Hellenism are all that we shall see; —at one time, the indestructible religious experience of mankind asserting itself blindly; at another, a revulsion of the intellect of mankind from this experience, because of the audacious assumptions and gross inaccuracies with which men's account of it is intermingled.

At present it is such a revulsion which seems chiefly imminent. Give the churches of Nonconformity free scope, cries an ardent Congregationalist, and we will renew the wonders of the first times; we will confront this modern bugbear of physical science, show how hollow she is, and how she contradicts herself! In his mind's eye, this Nonconforming enthusiast already sees Professor Huxley in a white sheet, brought up at the Surrey Tabernacle between two deacons,—whom that great physicist, in his own clear and nervous language, would no doubt describe as like his disinterred Roman the other day at Westminster Abbey, 'of weak mental organisation and strong muscular frame,'—and penitently confessing that *Science contradicts herself.* Alas, the real future is likely to be very different! Rather are we likely to witness an edifying solemnity, where Mr. Mill, assisted by his youthful henchmen and apparitors, will burn all the Prayer Books. Rather will the time come, as it has been foretold, when we shall desire to see one of the days of the Son of Man, and shall not see it; when the mildness and sweet reasonableness of Jesus Christ, as a power to work the annulment of our ordinary self, will be clean disregarded and out of mind. Then, perhaps, will come another reaction, and another, and another; and all sterile.

Therefore it is, that we labour to make Hebraism raise itself above Mialism, find its true self, show itself in its beauty and power, and help, not hinder, man's totality. The endeavour will very likely be in vain; for growth is slow and the ages are long, and it may well be that for harmonising Hebraism with Hellenism more preparation is needed than man has yet had. But failures do something, as well as successes, towards the final achievement. The cup of cold water could be hardly more than an ineffective effort at succour; yet it counted. To disengage the religion of England from unscriptural Protestantism, political Dissent, and a spirit of watchful jealousy, may be an aim not in our day reachable; and still it is well to level at it.

A COMMENT ON CHRISTMAS.

BISHOP WILSON is full of excellent things, and one of his apophthegms came into my mind the other day as I read an angry and unreasonable expostulation addressed to myself. Bishop Wilson's apophthegm is this: *Truth provokes those whom it does not convert.* 'Miracles,' I was angrily reproached for saying, 'do not happen, and more and more of us are becoming convinced that they do not happen; nevertheless, what is really best and most valuable in the Bible is independent of miracles, and for the sake of this, I constantly read the Bible myself, and I advise others to read it also.' One would have thought that at a time when the French newspapers are attributing all our failures and misfortunes to our habit of reading the Bible, and when our own Lieutenant-Governor of Bengal is protesting that the golden rule is a delusion and a snare for practical men, the friends of the old religion of Christendom would have had a kindly feeling towards anyone,—whether he admitted miracles or not,—who maintained that the root of the matter for all of us was in the Bible, and that to the use of the Bible we should still cling. But no; *Truth provokes those whom it does not convert.* So angry are some good people at being told that miracles do not happen, that if we say this, they cannot bear to have us using the Bible at all, or recommending the Bible. Either take it and recommend it with its miracles, they say, or else leave it alone, and let its enemies find confronting them none but orthodox defenders of it like ourselves.

The success of these orthodox champions is not at all commensurate with their zeal; and so, in spite of rebuke, I find myself, as a lover of the Bible, perpetually tempted to substitute for their line of defence a different method, however it may provoke them. Christmas comes round again, and brings the most beautiful and beloved festival of the Christian year. What is Christmas, and what does it say to us? Our French friends will reply that Christmas is an exploded legend, and says to us nothing at all. The *Guardian*, on the other hand, lays it down that Christmas commemorates the miracle of the Incarnation and that the truth of this miracle is the fundamental truth for Christians. Which is right, the *Guardian* or our French friends? Or are neither the one nor the other of them right, and is the truth about Christmas something quite different from what either of them imagine? The enquiry is profitable; and I kept Christmas, this last winter, by following it.

Who can ever lose out of his memory the roll and march of those magnificent words of prophecy, which, ever since we can remember, we have heard read in church on Christmas-day, and have been taught to regard as the grand and wonderful prediction of 'the miracle of the Incarnation?' 'The Lord himself shall give you a sign: Behold, a virgin shall conceive, and bear a son, and shall call his name Immanuel. Butter and honey shall he eat, until he shall know to refuse the evil and choose the good. For before the child shall know to refuse the evil and choose the good, the land that thou abhorrest shall be forsaken of both her kings.

We all know the orthodox interpretation. Immanuel is Jesus Christ, to be born of the Virgin Mary; the meaning of the name Immanuel, *God with us*, signifies the union of the divine nature and ours in Christ, God and man in one Person. 'Butter and honey shall he eat,'—the Christ shall be very man, he shall have a true human body, he shall be sustained, while he is growing up, with that ordinary nourishment wherewith human children are wont to be fed. And the sign that the promised birth of Immanuel, God and man in one Person, from the womb of a virgin, shall really happen, is this: the two kings of Syria and Israel who are now, in the eighth century before Christ, threatening the kingdom of Judah, shall be overthrown, and their country devastated. '*For* before the child shall know,'—before this promised coming of Jesus Christ, and as a sign to guarantee it, the kings of Syria and Israel shall be conquered and overthrown. And conquered and overthrown they presently were.

But then comes the turn of criticism. The study of history, and of all documents on which history is based, is diligently prosecuted; a number of learned, patient, impartial investigators read and examine the prophets. It becomes apparent what the prophets really mean to say. It becomes certain that in the famous words read on Christmas-day the prophet Isaiah was not meaning to speak of Jesus Christ to be born more than seven centuries later. It becomes certain that his Immanuel is a prince of Judah to be born in a year or two's time. It becomes certain that there is no question at all of a child miraculously conceived and born of a virgin. What the prophet declares is that a young woman, a damsel, at that moment unmarried, shall have time, before certain things happen, to be married and to bear a son, who shall be called Immanuel. There is no question in the name *Immanuel* of a union of the human and divine natures, of God and man in one Person. 'God present with his people and protecting them' is what the prophet means the name to signify. In 'Butter and honey shall he eat,' there is no question of the Christ's being very man, with a true human body. What the prophet intends to say is, that when the prince Immanuel, presently to be born, reaches adult age, agriculture shall have ceased in the desolated realm of Judah itself; the land, overrun by enemies, shall have returned to a wild state, the inhabitants shall live on the produce of their herds and on wild honey. But before this comes to pass, before the visitation of God's wrath upon the kingdom of Judah, and while the prince Immanuel is still but a little child, not as yet able to discern betwixt good and evil, 'to refuse the evil and choose the good,' the present enemies of Judah, the kings of Syria and Israel, shall be overthrown and their land made desolate. Finally, this overthrow and desolation are not, with the prophet, the sign and guarantee of Immanuel's coming. Immanuel is himself intended as a sign; all the rest is accompaniment of this sign, not proof of it.

This, the true and sure sense of those noble words of prophecy which we hear read on Christmas-day, is obscured by slight errors in the received translation, and comes out clearer when the errors are corrected:—

'The Lord himself shall give you a sign: Behold, the damsel shall conceive, and bear a son, and shall call his name Immanuel.

'Milk-curd and honey shall he eat, when he shall know to refuse the evil and choose the good.

'For before the child shall know to refuse the evil and choose the good, the land shall be forsaken, whose two kings make thee afraid.'

Syria and Israel shall be made desolate in Immanuel's infancy, says the prophet; but the chastisement and desolation of Judah also, he declares, shall follow later, by the time

Immanuel is a youth. Farther yet, however, Isaiah carries his prophecy of Immanuel and of the events of his life. In his manhood, the prophet continues, Immanuel, the promised child of the royal house of David, shall reign in righteousness over a restored, far-spreading, prosperous, and peaceful kingdom of the chosen people. 'Of the increase of his government and peace there shall be no end, upon the throne of David, and upon his kingdom.' This completion of the prophecy, too, we hear read in church on Christmas-day. Naturally, the received and erroneous interpretation, which finds, as we have seen, in the first part of the prophecy 'the miracle of the Incarnation,' governs our understanding of the latter part also. But in the latter part, as well as in the former, the prophet undoubtedly has in view, not a scion of the house of David to be born and to reign seven centuries later, but a scion of the house of David to be born immediately; a scion who in his youth should see Judah afflicted, in his manhood should reign over Judah restored and triumphant.

Well, then, the 'miracle of the Incarnation,' the preternatural conception and birth of Jesus Christ, which the Church celebrates at Christmas, and which is, says the *Guardian*, the fundamental truth for Christians, gets no support at all from the famous prophecy which is commonly supposed to announce it. Need I add that it gets no support at all from any single word of Jesus Christ himself, from any single word in the letters of Paul, Peter, James, or John? The miraculous conception and birth of Jesus is a *legend*, a lovely and attractive legend, which soon formed itself, naturally and irresistibly, around the origin of the Saviour; a legend which by the end of the first century had established itself, and which passed into two out of the four Gospel narratives that in the century following acquired canonicity. In the same way, a precisely similar legend formed itself around the origin of Plato, although to the popular imagination Plato was an object incomparably less fitted to offer stimulus. The father of Plato, said the Athenian story, was upon his marriage warned by Apollo in a dream that his wife, Perictiona, was about to bring forth a babe divinely conceived, and that he was to live apart from her until the child had been born. Among the students of philosophy, who were Plato's disciples, this story, although authorised by his family, languished and died. Had Plato founded a popular religion the case would have been very different. Then the legend would have survived and thriven; and for Plato, too, there would have certainly been a world-famous 'miracle of the Incarnation' investing his origin. But Plato, as Bossuet says, formed fewer disciples than Paul formed churches. It was these churches, this multitude, it was the popular masses with their receptivity, their love of wonders, with all their favouring native tendencies of mind, heart, and soul, which made the future of the Christian legend of the miracle of the Incarnation.

But because the story of the miracle of the Incarnation is a legend, and because two of the canonical Gospels propound the legend seriously, basing it upon an evidently fantastic use of the words of prophecy, and because the festival of Christmas adopts and consecrates this legend, are we to cast the Gospels aside, and cast the celebration of Christmas aside; or else are we to give up our reason and common sense, and to say that things are not what they are, and that Isaiah really predicted the preternatural conception and birth of Jesus Christ, and that the miracle of the Incarnation really happened as the *Guardian* supposes, and that Christians, in commemorating it, commemorate a solid fact of history, and a fact which is the fundamental truth for Christians? By no means. The solid fact of history marked by Christmas is the birth of Jesus, the miraculous circumstances with which that birth is invested and presented are legendary. The solid fact in itself, the birth of Jesus with its inexhaustible train of consequences, its 'unspeakable riches,' is foundation enough, and more than enough, for the Christmas festival; yet even the legend and miracle investing the fact, and now almost inseparable from it, have, moreover, their virtue of symbol.

Symbol is a dangerous word, and we ought to be very cautious in employing it. People have a difficulty in owning that a thing is unhistorical, and often they try to get out of the difficulty by saying that the thing is symbolical. Thus they think to save the credit of whoever delivered the thing in question, as if he had himself intended to deliver it as symbolical and figurative, not as historical. They save it, however, at the expense of truth. In very many cases undoubtedly, when this shift of symbol is resorted to for saving the credit of a narrator of legend, the narrator had not himself the least notion that what he propounded was figure, but fully imagined himself to be propounding historical fact. The Gospel narrators of the miracle of the Incarnation were in this position of mind; they did not in the least imagine themselves to be speaking symbolically. Nevertheless, a thing may have important value as symbol, although its utterer never told or meant it symbolically. Let us see how this is so with the Christian legend of the Incarnation.

In times and among minds where science is not a power, and where the preternatural is daily and familiarly admitted, the pureness and elevation of a great teacher strike powerfully the popular imagination, and the natural, simple, reverential explanation of his superiority is at once that he was born of a virgin. Such a legend is the people's genuine construing of the fact of his unique pureness. In his birth, as well as in his life and teaching, this chosen one has been pure,—has been unlike other men, and above them. Signal and splendid is the pureness of Plato; noble his serene faith, that 'the conclusion has long been reached that dissoluteness is to be condemned, in that it brings about the aggrandisement of the lower side in our nature, and the defeat of the higher.' And this lofty pureness of Plato impressed the imagination of his contemporaries, and evoked the legend of his having been born of a virgin. But Plato was, as I have already said, a philosopher, not the founder of a religion; his personality survived, but for the intellect mainly, not for the affections and imagination. It influenced and affected the few, not the many,—not the masses which love and foster legend. On the figure of Jesus also the stamp of a pureness unique and divine was seen to dwell. The remark has often been made that the pre-eminent, the winning, the irresistible Christian virtues, were charity and chastity. Perhaps the chastity was an even more winning virtue than the charity; it offered to the Pagan world, at any rate, relief from a more oppressive, a more consuming, a more intolerable bondage. Chief among the beatitudes, shone, no doubt, this pair: *Blessed are the poor in spirit, for theirs is the kingdom of heaven*, and, *Blessed are the pure in heart, for they shall see God*; and of these two, the second blessing may have brought even the greater boon. Jesus, then, the bestower of this precious blessing, Jesus, the high exemplar and ideal of pureness, was born of a virgin. And what Jesus brought was not a philosophy, but a religion; he gave not to the few, but to the masses, to the very recipients whom the tender legend of his being born of the gracious Virgin, and laid in the humble manger, would suit best; who might most surely be trusted to seize upon it, not to let it go, to delight in it and magnify it for ever.

So the legend of the miraculous conception and birth of Jesus, like the legend of the miraculous conception and birth of Plato, is the popular homage to a high ideal of pureness, it is the multitude's way of expressing for this its reverence. Of such reverence the legend is a genuine symbol. But the importance of the symbol is proportional to the scale on which it acts. And even when it acts on a very large scale, still its virtue will depend on these two things further : the worth of the idea to which it does homage, and the extent to which its recipients have succeeded in penetrating through the form of the legend to this idea.

And first, then, as to the innate truth and worth of that idea of pureness to which the legend of the miracle of the Incarnation does homage. *Blessed are the pure in heart, for they shall see God,* says Jesus. *God hath not called us to impureness, but unto holiness,* adds his apostle. Perhaps there is no doctrine of Christianity which is exposed to more trial amongst us now, certainly there is none which will be exposed, so far as from present appearances one can judge, to more trial in the immediate future, than this. *Let us return to nature,* is a rising and spreading cry again now, as it was at the Renascence. And the Christian pureness has so much which seems to contradict nature, and which is menaced by the growing desire and determination to return to nature ! The virtue has suffered more than most virtues in the hands of hypocrites ; and with hypocrites and hypocrisy, as a power in human life, there is an increasing impatience. But the virtue has been mishandled, also, by the sincere ; by the sincere, but who are at the same time over-rigid, formal, sour, narrow-minded ; and these, too, are by no means in the ascendant among us just now. Evidently, again, the virtue has been mishandled by many of the so-called saints, and by the asceticism of the Catholic Church ; for these have so managed things, very often, as to turn and rivet the thoughts upon the very matter from which pureness would avert them and get them clear, and have to that extent served to endanger and impair the virtue rather than forward it. Then, too, with the growing sense that gaiety and pleasure are legitimate demands of our nature, that they add to life and to our sum of force, instead of, as strict people have been wont to say, taking from it,—with this growing sense comes also the multiplication everywhere of the means of gaiety and pleasure, the spectacle ever more prominent of them and catching the eye more constantly, an ever larger number of applicants pressing forward to share in them. All this solicits the senses, makes them bold, eager, and stirring. At the same time the force of old sanctions of self-restraint diminishes and gives way. The belief in a magnified and non-natural man, out of our sight, but proved by miracles to exist and to be all-powerful, who by his commands has imposed on us the obligation of self-restraint, and who will punish us after death in endless fire if we disobey, will reward us in Paradise if we submit,—this belief is rapidly and irrecoverably losing its hold on men's minds. If pureness or any other virtue is still to subsist, it must subsist nowadays not by authority of this kind enforcing it in defiance of nature, but because nature herself turns out to be really for it.

Mr. Traill has reminded us, in the interesting volume on Coleridge which he has recently published, how Coleridge's disciple, Mr. Green, devoted the last years of his life to elaborating, in a work entitled *Spiritual Philosophy founded on the Teaching of the late Samuel Taylor Coleridge*, the great Coleridgian position 'that Christianity, rightly understood, is identical with the highest philosophy, and that, apart from all question of historical evidence, the essential doctrines of Christianity are necessary and eternal truths of reason,—truths which man, by the vouchsafed light of nature and without aid from documents or tradition, may always and everywhere discover for himself.' We shall not find this position established or much elucidated in *Spiritual Philosophy*. We shall not find it established or much elucidated in the works of Coleridge's immediate disciples. It was a position of extreme novelty to take at that time. Firmly to occupy it, resolutely to maintain it, required great boldness and great lucidity. Coleridge's position made demands upon his disciples which at that time it was almost impossible they should fulfil; it embarrassed them, forced them into vagueness and obscurity. The most eminent and popular among them, Mr. Maurice, seems never quite to have himself known what he himself meant, and perhaps never really quite wished to know. But neither did the master, as I have already said, establish his own position; there were obstacles in his own character, as well as obstacles in his circumstances, in the time. Nevertheless it is rightly called 'the great Coleridgian position.' It is at the bottom of all Coleridge's thinking and teaching; it is true; it is deeply important; and by virtue of it Coleridge takes rank, so far as English thought is concerned, as an initiator and founder. The 'great Coleridgian position,' that apart from all question of the evidence for miracles and of the historical quality of the Gospel narratives, the essential matters of Christianity are necessary and eternal facts of nature or truths of reason, is henceforth the key to the whole defence of Christianity. When a Christian virtue is presented to us as obligatory, the first thing, therefore, to be asked, is whether our need of it is a fact of nature.

Here the appeal is to experience and testimony. His own experience may in the end be the surest teacher for every man; but meanwhile, to confirm or deny his instinctive anticipations and to start him on his way, testimony as to the experience of others, general experience, is of the most serious weight and value. We have had the testimony of Plato to the necessity of pureness, that virtue on which

Christianity lays so much stress. Here is yet another testimony out of the same Greek world,—a world so alien to the world in which Christianity arose; here is the testimony of Sophocles. 'Oh that my lot might lead me in the path of holy *pureness* of thought and deed, the path which august laws ordain, laws which in the highest heaven had their birth; .... the power of God is mighty in them, and groweth not old.' That is the testimony of the poet Sophocles. Coming down to our own times, we have again a like testimony from the greatest poet of our times, Goethe; a testimony the more important, because Goethe, like Sophocles, was in his own life what the world calls by no means a purist. 'May the idea of *pureness*,' says Goethe, 'extending itself even to the very morsel which I take into my mouth, become ever clearer and more luminous within me!'

But let us consult the testimony not only of people far over our heads, such as great poets and sages; let us have the testimony of people living, as the common phrase is, in the world, and living there on an every-day footing. And let us choose a world the least favourable to purists possible, the most given to laxity,—and where indeed by this time the reign of the great goddess Lubricity seems, as I have often said, to be almost established,—the world of Paris. Two famous women of that world of Paris in the seventeenth century, two women not altogether unlike in spirit, Ninon de l'Enclos and Mme. de Sévigné, offer, in respect to the virtue with which we are now occupied, the most striking contrast possible. Both had, in the highest degree, freedom of spirit and of speech, boldness, gaiety, lucidity. Mme. de Sévigné, married to a worthless husband, then a widow, beautiful, witty, charming, of extraordinary freedom, easy and broad in her judgments, fond of enjoyment, not seriously religious,—Mme. de Sévigné, living in a society where almost everybody had a lover, never took one. The French commentators upon their incomparable country-woman are puzzled by this. But really the truth is, that not from what is called high moral principle, not from religion, but from sheer elementary soundness of nature and by virtue of her perfect lucidity, she revolted from the sort of life so common all around her, was drawn towards regularity, felt antipathy to blemish and disorder. Ninon, on the other hand, with a like freedom of mind, a like boldness and breadth in her judgments, a like gaiety and love of enjoyment, took a different turn, and her irregular life was the talk of her century. But that lucidity, which even all through her irregular life was her charm, made her say at the end of it: 'All the world tells me that I have less cause to speak ill of time than other people. However that may be, could anybody have proposed to me beforehand the life I have had, I would have hanged myself.' That, I say, is the testimony of the most lucid children of this world, as the testimony of Plato, Sophocles, and Goethe is the testimony of the loftiest spirits, to the natural obligation and necessity of the essentially Christian virtue of pureness. So when legend represents the founder of Christianity and great exemplar of this virtue as *born of a virgin*, thus doing homage to pureness, it does homage to what has natural worth and necessity.

But we have further to ask to what extent the recipients of the legend showed themselves afterwards capable, while firmly believing the legend and delighting in it, of penetrating to that virtue which it honoured, and of showing their sense that accompanying the legend went the glorification of that virtue. Here the Collects of the Church which have come down to us from Catholic antiquity,—from the times when all legend was most unhesitatingly received, most fondly loved, most delighted in for its own sake,—are the best testimony. Now the Collect for Christmas-day,—

that very day on which the miracle of the Incarnation is commemorated, and on which we might expect the legend's miraculous side to be altogether dominant,— firmly seizes the homage to pureness and renovation which is at the heart of the legend, and holds it steadily before us all Christmas-time. 'Almighty God,' so the Collect runs, 'who hast given us thine only-begotten Son to take our nature upon him, and as at this time to be born of a pure virgin, grant that we being regenerate, and made thy children through adoption and grace, may daily be renewed by thy Holy Spirit.'[1] The miracle is amply and impressively stated, but the stress is laid upon the work of regeneration and inward renewal, whereby we are to be made sons of God, like to that supreme Son whose pureness was expressed through his being born of a pure virgin. It is as, in celebrating at Easter the miracle of the Resurrection, the Church, following here St. Paul, seizes and elevates in the Collect for Easter Eve [2] that great 'secret of Jesus' which underlies the whole miraculous legend of the Resurrection, but which could arrive at the general heart of mankind only through materialising itself in that legend.

So manifest is it that there is that true and grand and profound doctrine of the *necrosis*, of 'dying to re-live,' underlying all which is legendary in the presentation of the death and resurrection of Jesus by our Gospels,—so manifest is it that St. Paul seized upon the doctrine and elevated it, and that the Church has retained it,—that one can find no difficulty, when the festival of Easter is celebrated, in

---

[1] The point in the Collect is taken from the Mozarabic Breviary at Lauds : 'Nos a mundanis contagiis munda, et in hoc mundo mundos nos esse constitue.'

[2] The point here is taken from a Benediction of St. Gregory for the First Sunday in Easter : 'Resuscitet vos de vitiorum sepulchris qui eum resuscitavit a mortuis.' See Blunt's *Annotated Book of Common Prayer*.

fixing one's thoughts upon the doctrine as a centre, and in receiving all the miraculous story as poetry naturally investing this and doing homage to it. But there is hardly a fast or a festival of the Christian year in which the underlying truth, the beneficent and forwarding idea, clothed with legend and miracle because mankind could only appropriate it by materialising it in legend and miracle, is not apparent. Trinity Sunday is an exception, but then Trinity Sunday does not really deal with Gospel story and miracle, it deals with speculation by theologians on the divine nature. Perhaps, considering the results of their speculation, we ought now rather to keep Trinity Sunday as a day of penitence for the aberrations of theological dogmatists. It is, however, in itself admissible and right enough that in the Christian year one day should be given to considering the aspects by which the human mind can in any degree apprehend God. But Trinity Sunday is, as I have said, an exception. For the most part, in the days and seasons which the Church observes, there is commemoration of some matter declared in Scripture, and combined and clothed more or less with miracle. Yet how near to us, under the accompanying investment of legend, does the animating and fructifying idea lie!—in Lent, with the miracle of the temptation, the idea of self-conquest and self-control; in Whitsuntide, with the miracle of the tongues of fire, the idea of the spirit and of inspiration.

What Christmas primarily commemorates is the birthday of Jesus,—Jesus, the bringer to the world of the new dispensation contained in his method and secret, and in his temper of sweet reasonableness for applying these. But the religion of Christendom has in fact made the prominent thing in Christmas a miracle, a legend; the miracle of the Incarnation, as it is called, the legend of Jesus having been born of a virgin. And to those who cannot bring themselves to receive miracle and legend as fact, what Christmas, under this popularly established aspect of it, can have to say to us, what significance it can contain, may at first sight seem doubtful. Christmas might at first appear to be the one great festival which is concerned wholly with mere miracle, which fixes our attention upon a miracle and nothing else. But when we come to look closer, we find that even in the case of Christmas the thing is not so. That on which Christmas, even in its popular acceptation, fixes our attention, is that to which the popular instinct, in attributing to Jesus his miraculous Incarnation, in believing him born of a pure Virgin, did homage :—pureness. And this to which the popular instinct thus did homage, was an essential characteristic of Jesus and an essential virtue of Christianity, the obligation of which, though apt to be questioned and discredited in the world, is at the same time nevertheless a necessary fact of nature and eternal truth of reason. And fondly as the Church has cherished and displayed the Christmas miracle, this, the true significance of the miraculous legend for religion, has never, the Christmas Collect shows us, been unknown to her, never wholly lost out of sight. As time goes on, as legend and miracle are less taken seriously as matters of fact, this worth of the Christmas legend as symbol will more and more come into view. The legend will still be loved, but as poetry,—as poetry endeared by the associations of some two thousand years; religious thought will rest upon that which the legend symbolises.

It is a mistake to suppose that rules for conduct and recommendations of virtue, presented in a correct scientific statement, or in a new rhetorical statement from which old errors are excluded, can have anything like the effect on mankind of old rules and recommendations to which we have been long accustomed, and with which our feelings and affections have become intertwined. Pedants always suppose that they can, but that this mistake should be so commonly made, proves only how many of us have a mixture of the pedant in our composition. A correct scientific statement of rules of virtue has upon the great majority of mankind simply no effect at all. A new rhetorical statement of them, appealing, like the old familiar deliverances of Christianity, to the heart and imagination, can have the effect which those deliverances had, only when they proceed from a religious genius equal to that from which those proceeded. To state the requirement is to declare the impossibility of its being satisfied. The superlative pedantry of Comte is shown in his vainly imagining that he could satisfy it; the comparative pedantry of his disciples is shown by the degree in which they adopt their master's vain imagination.

The really essential ideas of Christianity have a truth, depth, necessity, and scope, far beyond anything that either the adherents of popular Christianity, or its impugners, at present suppose. Jesus himself, as I have remarked elsewhere, is even the better fitted to stand as the central figure of a religion, because his reporters so evidently fail to comprehend him fully and to report him adequately. Being so evidently great and yet so uncomprehended, and being now inevitably so to remain for ever, he thus comes to stand before us as what the philosophers call an *absolute*. We cannot apply to him the tests which we can apply to other phenomena, we cannot get behind him and above him, cannot command him. But even were Jesus less of an *absolute*, less fitted to stand as the central figure of a religion than he is, even were the constitutive and essential ideas of Christianity less pregnant, profound, and far-reaching than they are, still the personage of Jesus, and the Christian rules of conduct and recommendations of virtue, being of that indisputable significance and worth which in any fair view to be taken of them they are, and also so widely known and loved from of old, would have a value and a substantiality for religious purposes which no new apparitions and constructions can possibly have. No new constructions in religion can now hope to found a common way, hold aloft a common truth, unite men in a common life. And yet how true it is, in regard to mankind's conduct and course, that, as the *Imitation* says so admirably, 'Without a way there is no going, without a truth, no knowing, without a life, no living.' *Sine viâ non itur, sine veritate non cognoscitur, sine vitâ non vivitur.* The way, truth, and life have been found in Christianity, and will not now be found outside of it. Instead of making vain and pedantic endeavours to invent them outside of it, what we have to do is to help, so far as we can, towards their continuing to be found inside of it by honest and sane people, who would be glad to find them there if they can accomplish it without playing tricks with their understanding; to help them to accomplish this, to remove obstacles out of the way of their doing so.

Far from having anything to gain by being timid and reticent, or else vague and rhetorical, in treating of the miraculous element in the Bible, he who would help men will probably now do most good by treating this element with entire unreserve. Let him frankly say, that miracle narrated in the Bible is as legendary as miracle narrated anywhere else, and not more to be taken as having actually happened. If he calls it symbolical, let him be careful to admit that the narrators did not mean it for symbol, but delivered it as having actually happened, and in so delivering it were mistaken. Let him say that we can still use it as poetry, and that in so using it we use it better than those who used it as matter of fact; but let him not leave in any uncertainty the point that it is as poetry that we do use it.

Let no difficulties be slurred over or eluded. Undoubtedly a period of transition in religious belief, such as the period in which we are now living, presents many grave difficulties. Undoubtedly the reliance on miracles is not lost without some danger; but the thing to consider is that it *must* be lost, and that the danger must be met, and, as it can be, counteracted.

If men say, as some men are likely enough to say, that they altogether give up Christian miracles and cannot do otherwise, but that then they give up Christian morals too, the answer is, that they do this at their own risk and peril; that they need not do it, that they are wrong in doing it, and will have to rue their error. But for my part, I prefer at present to affirm this reality of Christian morals simply and barely, not to give any rhetorical development to it. Springs of interest for the emotions and feelings that reality possesses in abundance, and hereafter these springs may and will most beneficially be used by the clergy and teachers of religion, who are the best persons to turn them to account. As they have habitually and powerfully used the springs of emotion contained in the Christian legend, so they will with time come to use the springs of emotion contained in the Christian reality. But there has been so much vagueness, and so much rhetoric, and so much licence of affirmation, and so much treatment of what cannot be known as if it were well known, and of what is poetry and legend as if it were essential solid fact, and of what is investment and dress of the matter as if it were the heart of the matter, that for the present, and when we are just at the commencement of a new departure, I prefer, I say, to put forward a plain, strict statement of the essential facts and truths consecrated by the Christian legend, and to confine myself to doing this. No doubt, not even those facts and truths can produce their full effect upon men when exhibited in a mere naked statement. Nevertheless, the most important service we can render to Christianity, at the present moment, is perhaps not so much to work upon men's feelings with rhetoric about it, as to show to their understandings what its essential facts and truths really are.

Therefore, when we are asked: What really is Christmas, and what does it celebrate? we answer: The birthday of Jesus. But what, then, is the miracle of the Incarnation? A homage to the virtue of pureness, and to the manifestation of this virtue in Jesus. What is Lent, and the miracle of the temptation? A homage to the virtue of self-control and to the manifestation of this virtue in Jesus. What does Easter celebrate? Jesus victorious over death by dying. By dying how? Dying to re-live. To re-live in Paradise, in another world? No, in this. But if in this, what is the kingdom of God? The ideal society of the future. Then what is immortality? To live in the eternal order, which never dies. What is salvation by Jesus Christ? The attainment of this immortality. Through what means? Through faith in Jesus, and appropriation of his method, secret, and temper.

Men's experience of the saving results of the method and secret and temper of Jesus, imperfectly even as his method and secret and temper have been extricated and employed hitherto, makes truly the strength of that wonderful Book, in which, with an immense vehicle of legend and miracle, the new dispensation of Jesus and the old dispensation which led up to it are exhibited and brought to mankind's knowledge; makes the strength of the Bible, and of the religion and churches which the Bible has called into being. We may remark that what makes the attraction of a church is always what is consonant in it to the method and secret and temper of Jesus, and productive, therefore, of the saving results which flow from these. The attraction of the

Catholic Church is unity; of the Protestant sects, conscience; of the Church of England, abuses reformed but unity saved. I speak of that which, in each of these cases, is the attraction, the promise apparently held out; I do not say that the promise is made good. The attraction, in each case, is something given by the line of Jesus. That which makes the weakness and danger of a church, again, is just that in it which is not consonant to the line of Jesus. Thus the danger of the Catholic Church is its obscurantism; of the Protestant sects, their contentiousness; of the Church of England, its deference to station and property. I said in a discourse at the East-end of London that ever since the appearance of Christianity *the prince of this world is judged.* The *Guardian* was much alarmed at my saying that, and reproved me for saying it. I will urge nothing in answer, except that this deference to the *prince of this world*, to the susceptibilities of station and property, which has been too characteristic of the Church of England in the past,—a deference so signally at variance with the line of Jesus,—is at the same time just what now makes the Church of England's weakness and main danger.

As time goes on, it will be more and more manifest that salvation does really depend on conformity to the line of Jesus; and that this experience, and nothing miraculous or preternatural, is what establishes the truth and necessity of Christianity. The experience proceeds on a large scale, and therefore slowly. But even now, and imperfectly moreover as the line of Jesus has been followed hitherto, it can be seen that those nations are the soundest which have the most seriously concerned themselves with it and have most endeavoured to follow it. Societies are saved by following it, broken up by not following it; and as the experience of this continually proceeds, the proofs of Christianity are continually accumulating and growing stronger. The thing goes on quite independently of our wishes, and whether we will or no. Our French neighbours seem perfectly and scornfully incredulous as to the cogency of the beatitude which pronounces blessing on the pure in heart; they would not for a moment admit that nations perish through the service of the great goddess Lubricity. On the contrary, more and more of them, great and small, philosophers as well as the vulgar, maintain this service to be the most natural and reasonable thing in the world. Yet really this service broke up the great Roman Empire in the past, and is capable, it will be found, of breaking up any number of societies.

Or let us consider that other great beatitude and its fortunes, the beatitude recommending the Christian virtue of charity: 'Blessed are the poor in spirit, for theirs is the kingdom of heaven.' Many people do not even understand what it is which this beatitude means to bless; they think it recommends humbleness of spirit. Ferdinand Baur, whose exegesis of texts from the Gospels is more valuable than his criticism of the mode in which the Gospels were composed, has very well pointed out that the persons here blest are not those who are humble-spirited, but those who are in the intention and bent of their spirit,—in mind, as we say, and not in profession merely,—indifferent to riches. Such persons, whether they possess riches or not, really regard riches as something foreign to them, something not their own, and are thus, in the phrase of another text where our received translation is misleading, *faithful* as regards riches. 'If ye have not been faithful in that which is foreign to you, who will give you that which is your own?' The faithfulness consists in having conquered the temptation to treat that for which men desire riches, private possession and personal enjoyment, as things vital to us and so be desired. Wherever there is cupidity, in short, there the blessing of the Gospel cannot rest. The actual poor, therefore, may altogether fail to be objects of that blessing, the actual rich may be objects of it in the highest degree. Nay, the surest of means to restore and perpetuate the reign of the selfish rich, if at any time it have been menaced or interrupted, is cupidity, envy, and hatred in the poor. And this, again, is a witness to the infallibility of the line of Jesus. We must come, both rich and poor, to prefer the common good, the interest of 'the body of Christ,'—to use the Gospel phrase,—the body of Christ of which we are members, to private possession and personal enjoyment.

This is Christian charity, and how rare, how very rare it is, we all know. In this practical country of ours, where possessing property and estate is so loved, and losing them so dreaded, the opposition to Christian charity is almost as strong as that to Christian purity in France. The *Saturday Review* is in general respectful to religion, sane in behaviour, in matters of criticism reasonable. But let it imagine property and privilege threatened, and instantly what a change ! There seems to rise before one's mind's eye a sort of vision of an elderly demoniac, surrounded by a troop of younger demoniacs of whom he is the owner and guide, all of them suddenly foaming at the mouth and crying out horribly. The attachment to property and privilege is so strong, the fear of losing them so agitating. But the line of Jesus perpetually tends to establish itself, as I have said, independently of our wishes, and whether we will or no. And undoubtedly the line of Jesus is : 'How hardly shall they that have riches enter into the kingdom of God !' In other words : 'How hardly shall those who cling to private possession and personal enjoyment, who have not brought themselves to regard property and riches as foreign and indifferent to them, who have not annulled self and placed their happiness in the common good, make part of the ideal society of the future !'

The legend of Christmas is a homage to the Christian

virtue of pureness; and Christmas, with its 'miracle of the Incarnation,' should turn our thoughts to the certainty of this virtue's final victory, against all difficulties. And with the victory of this virtue let us associate the victory of its great fellow-virtue of Christian charity, a victory equally difficult but equally certain. The difficulties are undeniable, but here, however, the signs of the times point far more to the emergence and progress of the virtue than to its depression. Who cannot see that the idea of the common good is acquiring amongst us, at the present day, a force altogether new? that for instance, in cases where, in the framing of laws and in the interpretation of them by tribunals, regard to property and privilege used to be, one may say, paramount, and the idea of the common good hardly considered at all, things are now tending quite the other way; the pretensions of property and privilege are severely scrutinised, the claims of the common good entertained with favour.

An acceleration of progress in the spread of ideas of this kind, a decline of vitality in institutions where the opposite ideas were paramount, marks the close of a period. Jesus announced for his own period such a close; a close necessitated by the emergence of the new, the decay of the old. He announced it with the turbid figures familiar through prophecy to his hearers' imagination, figures of stupendous physical miracle, a break-up of nature, God coming to judgment. But he did not announce under these figures, as our Bibles make him announce, the end of *the world*; he announced 'the end of *the age*,' 'the close of *the period*.' That close came, as he had foretold; and a like 'end of the age' is imminent, wherever a certain stage is reached in the conflict between the line of Jesus and the facts of that period through which it takes its passage. Sometimes we may almost be inclined to augur that from some such 'end of the age' we ourselves are not far distant now; that through dissolution

—dissolution peaceful if we have virtue enough, violent if we are vicious, but still dissolution,—we and our own age have to pass, according to the eternal law which makes dissolution the condition of renovation. The price demanded, according to the inexorable conditions on which the kingdom of God is offered, for the mistakes of our past, for the attainment of our future, this price may perhaps be required sooner than we suppose, required even of us ourselves who are living now : 'Verily I say unto you, it shall be required *of this generation.*'

SMITH, ELDER, & CO.'S PUBLICATIONS.

WORKS BY THE LATE MATTHEW ARNOLD.

PASSAGES FROM THE PROSE WRITINGS OF MATTHEW ARNOLD. Crown 8vo. 7s. 6d.
CONTENTS:—1. Literature.—2. Politics and Society.—3. Philosophy and Religion.

LAST ESSAYS ON CHURCH AND RELIGION. With a Preface. Crown 8vo. 7s.

MIXED ESSAYS. Second Edition. Crown 8vo. 9s.
CONTENTS:—Democracy—Equality—Irish Catholicism and British Liberalism—Porro Unum est Necessarium—A Guide to English Literature—Falkland—A French Critic on Milton—A French Critic on Goethe—George Sand.

LITERATURE AND DOGMA: an Essay towards a Better Apprehension of the Bible. Popular Edition, with a new Preface. Crown 8vo. 2s. 6d.

GOD AND THE BIBLE: a Sequel to 'Literature and Dogma.' Popular Edition, with a new Preface. Crown 8vo. 2s. 6d.

ST. PAUL AND PROTESTANTISM; with Other Essays. Popular Edition with a new Preface. Crown 8vo. 2s. 6d.
CONTENTS:—St. Paul and Protestantism—Puritanism and the Church of England—Modern Dissent—A Comment on Christmas.

CULTURE AND ANARCHY: an Essay in Political and Social Criticism. Popular Edition. Crown 8vo. 2s. 6d.

IRISH ESSAYS, AND OTHERS. Popular Edition. Cr. 8vo. 2s. 6d.

ON THE STUDY OF CELTIC LITERATURE. Popular Edition. Crown 8vo. 2s. 6d.

WORKS BY THE LATE GEORGE HENRY LEWES.

THE STORY OF GOETHE'S LIFE. Second Edition. Crown 8vo. cloth, 7s. 6d.; or, tree-calf, 12s. 6d.

THE LIFE OF GOETHE. Fourth Edition. With Portrait. 8vo. 16s.

STUDIES IN ANIMAL LIFE. With Coloured Frontispiece and other Illustrations. Crown 8vo. 5s.

ON ACTORS AND THE ART OF ACTING. Second Edition. Crown 8vo. 7s. 6d.

WORKS BY LESLIE STEPHEN.

LIFE OF HENRY FAWCETT. With 2 Steel Portraits. Fourth Edition. Large crown 8vo. 12s. 6d.

THE SCIENCE OF ETHICS; an Essay upon Ethical Theory, as Modified by the Doctrine of Evolution. Demy 8vo. 16s.

A HISTORY OF ENGLISH THOUGHT IN THE EIGHTEENTH CENTURY. Second Edition. 2 vols. Demy 8vo. 28s.

HOURS IN A LIBRARY. Second Series. Second Edition. Cr. 8vo. 9s.
CONTENTS:—Sir Thomas Browne—Jonathan Edwards—William Law—Horace Walpole—Dr. Johnson's Writings—Crabbe's Poetry—William Hazlitt—Mr. Disraeli's Novels.

London : SMITH, ELDER, & CO., 15 Waterloo Place.

SMITH, ELDER, & CO.'S PUBLICATIONS.

THE LIFE AND LETTERS OF ROBERT BROWNING. By Mrs. SUTHERLAND ORR. With Portrait, and Steel Engraving of Mr. Browning's Study in De Vere Gardens. Second Edition. Crown 8vo. 12s. 6d.

ENGLISH PROSE: its Elements, History and Usage. By JOHN EARLE, M.A., Rector of Swanswick, formerly Fellow and Tutor of Oriel College, Professor of Anglo-Saxon in the University of Oxford, Author of 'The Philology of the English Tongue,' &c. 8vo. 16s.

THE HISTORIC NOTE-BOOK ; with an Appendix of Battles. By the Rev. E. COBHAM BREWER, LL.D., Author of 'The Dictionary of Phrase and Fable,' 'The Reader's Handbook,' &c. Crown 8vo. over 1,000 pp., 10s. 6d.

WOODLAND, MOOR, AND STREAM; being the Notes of a Naturalist. Edited by J. A. OWEN. Second Edition. Crown 8vo. 5s.

FALLING IN LOVE; with other Essays treating of some more Exact Sciences. By GRANT ALLEN. Crown 8vo. 6s.

ROBERT ELSMERE. By Mrs. HUMPHRY WARD, Author of 'Miss Bretherton' &c. Cabinet edition, 2 vols. small 8vo. 12s.

*** Also the POPULAR EDITION, 1 vol. crown 8vo. 6s. ; and the CHEAP EDITION, crown 8vo. limp cloth, 2s. 6d.

GEOLOGICAL OBSERVATIONS ON THE VOLCANIC ISLANDS AND PARTS OF SOUTH AMERICA, visited during the Voyage of H.M.S. 'Beagle.' By CHARLES DARWIN, M.A., F.R.S. Third Edition. With Maps and Illustrations. Crown 8vo. 12s. 6d.

THE STRUCTURE AND DISTRIBUTION OF CORAL REEFS. By CHARLES DARWIN, M.A., F.R.S., F.G.S. With an Introduction by Professor T. G. BONNEY, D.Sc., F.R.S., F.G.S. Third Edition. Crown 8vo. 8s. 6d.

HAYTI ; or, the Black Republic. By Sir SPENSER ST. JOHN, K.C.M.G., formerly Her Majesty's Minister Resident and Consul-General in Hayti, now Her Majesty's Special Envoy to Mexico. Second Edition, revised. With a Map. Large crown 8vo. 8s. 6d.

THE REIGN OF QUEEN VICTORIA: a Survey of Fifty Years of Progress. Edited by T. HUMPHRY WARD. 2 vols. 8vo. 32s.

A COLLECTION OF LETTERS OF W. M. THACKERAY, 1847–1855. With Portraits and Reproductions of Letters and Drawings. Second Edition. Imperial 8vo. 12s. 6d.

LIFE OF FRANK BUCKLAND. By his Brother-in-Law, GEORGE C. BOMPAS, Editor of 'Notes and Jottings from Animal Life.' With a Portrait. Crown 8vo. 5s. ; gilt edges. 6s.

NOTES AND JOTTINGS FROM ANIMAL LIFE. By the late FRANK BUCKLAND. With Illustrations. Crown 8vo. 5s. ; gilt edges, 6s.

JESS. By H. RIDER HAGGARD, Author of 'King Solomon's Mines' &c. Crown 8vo. 2s. 6d.

VICE VERSÂ ; or, a Lesson to Fathers. By F. ANSTEY. Crown 8vo. 2s. 6d.

By the same Author.

A FALLEN IDOL. Crown 8vo. 2s. 6d. | **THE PARIAH.** Cr. 8vo. 6s. Cheap Edition, cr. 8vo. limp cloth, 2s. 6d.

THE GIANT'S ROBE. Crown 8vo. 6s.

MORE T LEAVES; a Collection of Pieces for Public Reading. By EDWARD F. TURNER, Author of 'T Leaves,' 'Tantler's Sister,' &c. Cr. 8vo. 4s. 6d.

By the same Author.

T LEAVES; a Collection of Pieces for Public Reading. Fifth Edition. Crown 8vo. 3s. 6d.

TANTLER'S SISTER ; AND OTHER UNTRUTHFUL STORIES: being a Collection of Pieces written for Public Reading. Third Edition. Crown 8vo. 3s. 6d.

London : SMITH, ELDER, & CO., 15 Waterloo Place.

W. M. THACKERAY'S WORKS

THE LIBRARY EDITION.

In Twenty-four Volumes, Large Crown 8vo. 7s. 6d. each, with Illustrations by the Author, RICHARD DOYLE, and FREDERICK WALKER. Sets in cloth, £9; or, in half-russia, £13. 13s.

VANITY FAIR. A NOVEL WITHOUT A HERO. Two Volumes. With Forty Steel Engravings and 150 Woodcuts.

THE HISTORY OF PENDENNIS: HIS FORTUNES AND MISFORTUNES: HIS FRIENDS AND HIS GREATEST ENEMY. Two Volumes. With Forty Steel Engravings and numerous Woodcuts.

THE NEWCOMES: MEMOIRS OF A MOST RESPECTABLE FAMILY. Two Volumes. With Forty-eight Steel Engravings by RICHARD DOYLE, and numerous Woodcuts.

THE HISTORY OF HENRY ESMOND, ESQ.: A COLONEL IN THE SERVICE OF HER MAJESTY QUEEN ANNE. With Eight Illustrations by GEORGE DU' MAURIER, and numerous Woodcuts.

THE VIRGINIANS: A TALE OF THE LAST CENTURY. Two Volumes. With Forty-eight Steel Engravings and numerous Woodcuts.

THE ADVENTURES OF PHILIP ON HIS WAY THROUGH THE WORLD, SHOWING WHO ROBBED HIM, WHO HELPED HIM, AND WHO PASSED HIM BY. To which is prefixed A SHABBY GENTEEL STORY. Two Volumes. With Twenty Illustrations.

THE PARIS SKETCH-BOOK OF MR. M. A. TITMARSH AND THE MEMOIRS OF MR. C. J. YELLOWPLUSH. With Illustrations by the Author.

THE MEMOIRS OF BARRY LYNDON, ESQ., WRITTEN BY HIMSELF: WITH THE HISTORY OF SAMUEL TITMARSH, AND THE GREAT HOGGARTY DIAMOND. With Illustrations by the Author.

THE IRISH SKETCH-BOOK: AND NOTES OF A JOURNEY FROM CORNHILL TO GRAND CAIRO. With Illustrations by the Author.

THE BOOK OF SNOBS; SKETCHES AND TRAVELS IN LONDON; AND CHARACTER SKETCHES. With Illustrations by the Author.

BURLESQUES:—
Novels by Eminent Hands—Adventures of Major Gahagan—Jeames's Diary—A Legend of the Rhine—Rebecca and Rowena—The History of the Next French Revolution—Cox's Diary. With Illustrations by the Author and RICHARD DOYLE.

CHRISTMAS BOOKS OF MR. A. TITMARSH:—
Mrs. Perkins's Ball—Dr. Birch—Our Street—The Kickleburys on the Rhine—The Rose and the Ring. With Seventy-four Illustrations by the Author.

BALLADS AND TALES. With Illustrations by the Author.

THE FOUR GEORGES; THE ENGLISH HUMORISTS OF THE EIGHTEENTH CENTURY. With Portraits and other Illustrations.

ROUNDABOUT PAPERS. To which is added the SECOND FUNERAL OF NAPOLEON. With Illustrations by the Author.

DENIS DUVAL; LOVEL THE WIDOWER; AND OTHER STORIES. With Illustrations by FREDERICK WALKER and the Author.

CATHERINE, a Story; LITTLE TRAVELS; THE FITZBOODLE PAPERS; CRITICAL REVIEWS; AND THE WOLVES AND THE LAMB. Illustrations by the Author, and a Portrait.

MISCELLANEOUS ESSAYS, SKETCHES, AND REVIEWS. With Illustrations by the Author.

CONTRIBUTIONS TO 'PUNCH.' With 132 Illustrations by the Author.

THE POPULAR EDITION.

Complete in Thirteen Volumes, Crown 8vo. with Frontispiece to each Volume, price 5s. each.

Sets, handsomely bound in scarlet cloth, gilt top, price £3. 5s.; or in half-morocco gilt, price £5. 10s.

1.—VANITY FAIR.
2.—THE HISTORY OF PENDENNIS.
3.—THE NEWCOMES.
4.—ESMOND AND BARRY LYNDON.
5.—THE VIRGINIANS.
6.—THE ADVENTURES OF PHILIP, to which is prefixed A SHABBY GENTEEL STORY.
7.—PARIS, IRISH, AND EASTERN SKETCHES:—
Paris Sketch Book—Irish Sketch Book—Cornhill to Cairo.
8.—HOGGARTY DIAMOND, YELLOWPLUSH PAPERS, AND BURLESQUES:—
The Great Hoggarty Diamond — Yellowplush Papers—Novels by Eminent Hands—Jeames's Diary—Adventures of Major Gahagan—A Legend of the Rhine—Rebecca and Rowena—The History of the Next French Revolution—Cox's Diary —The Fatal Boots.
9.—THE BOOK OF SNOBS, AND SKETCHES OF LIFE & CHARACTER:—
The Book of Snobs—Sketches and Travels in London—Character Sketches—Men's Wives—the Fitzboodle Papers—The Bedford Row Conspiracy—A Little Dinner at Timmins's.
10.—ROUNDABOUT PAPERS AND LECTURES:—
Roundabout Papers—The Four Georges—The English Humorists of the Eighteenth Century—The Second Funeral of Napoleon.
11.—CATHERINE, &c.
Catherine—Lovel the Widower—Denis Duval—Ballads—The Wolves and the Lamb—Critical Reviews—Little Travels and Roadside Sketches.
12.—CHRISTMAS BOOKS:—
Mrs. Perkins's Ball—Dr. Birch—Our Street—The Kickleburys on the Rhine—The Rose and the Ring.
13.—MISCELLANEOUS ESSAYS, SKETCHES, AND REVIEWS; CONTRIBUTIONS TO 'PUNCH.'

London: SMITH, ELDER, & CO., 15 Waterloo Place.

'A work absolutely indispensable to every well-furnished library.'—THE TIMES.

Price 15s. net per volume, in cloth; or in half-morocco, marbled edges, 20s. net.

DICTIONARY of NATIONAL BIOGRAPHY.

Edited by LESLIE STEPHEN and SIDNEY LEE.

Volume I. was published on January 1, 1885, *and a volume has been issued every three months since that date.*

A further Volume will be published on January 1, *April* 1, *July* 1, *and October* 1 *of each year until the completion of the work.*

EXTRACTS FROM A FEW RECENT PRESS NOTICES OF THE WORK.

TRUTH.—'I am glad you share my admiration for Mr. Stephen's *magnum opus*—THE MAGNUM OPUS OF OUR GENERATION—"The Dictionary of National Biography." A dictionary of the kind had been attempted so often before by the strongest men—publishers and editors—of the day that I hardly expected it to succeed. No one expected such a success as it has so far achieved.'

THE ATHENÆUM.—'The latest volumes of Mr. Stephen's Dictionary are FULL OF IMPORTANT AND INTERESTING ARTICLES. Great names strike the eye constantly as we turn the pages. . . . Altogether the volumes are good reading. What is more important, the articles, whether they are on small or great personages, are nearly all up to the high standard which has been set in the earlier portions of the work, and occasionally above it.'

SATURDAY REVIEW.—'From the names we have cited it will be seen that great pains have been taken with that portion of the Dictionary which relates to modern times, and this has been rightly done; for often nothing is more difficult than to find a concise record of the life of a man who belonged to our own times or to those just preceding them. Consistently enough, the Editor has been careful to keep the work reasonably up to date.'

THE MANCHESTER EXAMINER AND TIMES.—'This magnificent work of reference has now left the tentative stage of its existence far behind, and Mr. Leslie Stephen and his contributors are well under weigh. . . . We extend a hearty welcome to the latest instalment of a most magnificent work, in which both the editing and the writing appear still to improve.'

THE QUARTERLY REVIEW.—'A "DICTIONARY OF NATIONAL BIOGRAPHY," OF WHICH THE COUNTRY MAY BE JUSTLY PROUD, which, though it may need correcting and supplementing, will probably never be superseded, and which, in unity of conception and aim, in the number of the names inserted, in fulness and accuracy of details, in the care and precision with which the authorities are cited, and in the bibliographical information given, will not only be immeasurably superior to any work of the kind which has been produced in Great Britain, but will as far surpass the German and Belgian biographical dictionaries now in progress, as these two important undertakings are in advance of the two great French collections, which until lately reigned supreme in the department of Biography.'

THE LANCET.—'Its contents show no falling off in accuracy and completeness, so far as by a critical examination we have been able to discover, from those of the previous volumes, of which we have on all occasions spoken with praise. When completed, THE DICTIONARY WILL BE WELL NIGH INVALUABLE.

THE PALL MALL GAZETTE.—'As to the general execution, we can only repeat the high praise which it has been our pleasing duty to bestow on former volumes. To find a name omitted that should have been inserted is well-nigh impossible.'

THE GLASGOW HERALD —'It is not easy to overpraise a book, which, although bearing the unpretentious name of a dictionary, is not more perfect in design than comprehensive and admirable in execution. It is so useful as to be necessary in all libraries, public as well as private.'

London: SMITH, ELDER, & CO., 15 Waterloo Place.

www.ingramcontent.com/pod-product-compliance
Lightning Source LLC
Chambersburg PA
CBHW031444160426
43195CB00010BB/843